SO FULL OF SHAPES

A reading of
Shakespeare's *Twelfth Night*

Matt Simpson

GREENWICH EXCHANGE
LONDON

Greenwich Exchange, London

First published in Great Britain in 2006

Printed and bound by Q3 Digital/Litho, Loughborough
Tel: 01509 213456
Typesetting and layout by Albion Associates, London
Tel: 020 8852 4646
Cover design by December Publications, Belfast
Tel: 028 90352059

Cover: © ArenaPAL

Greenwich Exchange Website: www.greenex.co.uk

ISBN-13: 978-1-871551-86-0
ISBN-10: 1871551-86-2

for Geoff and Anna

I would like to express my thanks to Angela Topping and John Farrell for encouragement and friendship, to Professor John Lucas for his and also for his painstaking reading of the first draft, and to Monika for her patience.

Love can transpose to form and dignity.

A Midsummer Night's Dream

Love is a universal migraine,
A bright stain on the vision,
Blotting out reason.

Symptoms of true love
Are leanness, jealousy,
Laggard dawns.

Robert Graves

Journeys end in lovers meeting,
Every wise man's son doth know.

Feste's song in Twelfth Night

How shall we find the concord of this discord?

A Midsummer Night's Dream

Contents

Prologue – Are You a Comedian?   ix

1   But That's All One   1

2   What Is Love?   4

3   Like a Cloistress   11

4   One Heart, One Bosom, and One Truth   16

5   Give Me Some Music   19

6   To Time I Will Commit   23

7   Wit, and't Be Thy Will   28

8   Are All the People Mad?   33

9   I'll Serve This Duke   38

10 Conceal Me What I Am   45

11 Suppose Him Virtuous   49

12 Sometimes He is a Kind of Puritan   53

13 All is Semblative a Woman's Part   61

14 Corrupter of Words   64

15 Nay, I Am for All Waters   68

16 The Whirligig of Time   73

Epilogue – Hey, Ho   78

Bibliography   79

Prologue – Are You a Comedian?

Twelfth Night is sometimes referred to as a 'golden' or 'festive' comedy, though more usually it's described as 'romantic'. The simple reason for this being that the main theme is love, or, more accurately, the confusions of young lovers brought to happy conclusions – though, as Middleton Murry has pointed out, and many people feel, *Twelfth Night* has a 'silvery undertone of sadness' to it. These descriptions distinguish it from 'satirical' corrective comedy, in which the aim is to expose and ridicule corruption. Shakespeare's contemporary, Ben Jonson, in plays like *Volpone* and *The Alchemist*, is master of this kind of comedy – a kind that Renaissance theorists, such as Philip Sidney and George Puttenham in England, advocated as the only true type. It is said that Shakespeare, more concerned with entertaining and giving pleasure than wanting to reform, wrote every other kind of comedy but satirical. The adjective 'golden' is little more than descriptive, suggesting best-in-its-class and sunny in its disposition (a view running the risk of ignoring or undervaluing the play's darker aspects); 'festive' is more apposite, as the play's title and the name Feste – attaching it to the final day of the Christmas revels, a time of Misrule when the normal world was turned on its head – determines.

The mock self-deprecation of the subtitle is in keeping with the titles of other comedies like *Much Ado About Nothing* and *As You Like It*. But since there is nothing other than the title directly connecting the play with the end of the Christmas revels or with the Feast of Epiphany (in Act III, scene 4, Olivia actually says "Why, this is very midsummer madness" – Midsummer Eve being 23rd June), I have this fancy that someone who perhaps suggested or may have commissioned the play simply wanted it called *Twelfth Night* and Shakespeare's subtitle is like saying 'Okay, call it what you like,

I don't mind'. It signals that the audience is to expect a comedy and Shakespeare is pretending to hand over control of events to Time/ Fate … what you will. Perhaps it is as simple as Dover Wilson's assertion that *Twelfth Night* was first performed on that day.

Unfortunately the term 'comedy' has become blurred. In the way 'tragedy' is nowadays generally used to describe any unfortunate – and not necessarily fatal – event, so 'comedy' is used to denote whatever might be thought funny. Students of literature need to look for something more technical, even if the results of their findings inevitably contain – though hopefully fruitfully so – contradiction. In the medieval period comedy meant a poem in which a sad beginning turned into a happy ending, one that moved, as it were, out of shadow and into sunlight. Tragedy, by the same token, may be said to take an opposite direction. Chaucer in *The Monk's Tale* tells us:

> Tragedie is to seyn a certeyn storie
> As olde bokes make us memorie
> Of him that stood in greet prosperitie
> And is fallen out of heigh degree
> Into miserie, and endeth wrecchedly.

Olivia's question should give us pause: when she asks Cesario "Are you a comedian?" she actually means 'Are you an actor?' not 'Are you being funny?'

Putting comedy and tragedy into opposing camps has its drawbacks, among which is that of being persuaded the latter is a more profound expression of human truth and seeing the former– at worst – as something frivolous. Shakespeare's subtitle is a tease. In fact, comedy is more often than not a serious business, capable of providing insights as profound as those of tragedy. (Consider Blake's proverb "Excess of sorrow laughs. Excess of Joy weeps.") They are perhaps two sides of the same coin. Both try to show us what human beings are capable of, both concerned with exposing 'truth' and separating appearances from realities. Indeed some would argue that comedy has more to tell us about life, in that it's nearer to most people's quotidian experience, whereas tragedy may be said to deal with the intensified suffering of exceptional characters. In terms of style tragedy is held to be 'lofty' and comedy more 'earthbound'. But difference doesn't always denote superiority.

Comedy's effect on us has been and continues to be the subject of debate. As well as affording us opportunity to experience vicariously certain sympathies and accompany them with laughter, might it also allow us to indulge in feelings of superiority (you wouldn't catch me behaving like that, serves them right)? Does it allow us to evaluate things through effects of contrast and incongruity? Does it playfully exploit aroused expectations and then thwart them with surprise or disappointment and so release pent-up energies? Does it pleasingly satisfy our innate sense of justice by reaffirming what Maria calls "the modest limits of order"? Is it therefore conservative? In showing us what-is as distinct from what-ought-to-be, does it confirm societal values by restoring deviant behaviour to acceptable norms? If tragedy is about loss, comedy is surely about gain, about making adjustments, about realising that exercising commonsense is our best way of handling what the world throws at us, and about how we might forge proper relationships. It demonstrates that unreason is a form of madness, something that divides us from ourselves, and that what needs to be avoided is excess ("uncivil rule") in accordance – in this play at least – with Renaissance philosophy, rooted in the Greeks, which advocated the middle path, (the so-called "Golden Mean"), the avoidance of extremes, as the best route to the 'good life'.

Perhaps this summary of John Wain's may help:

> Anyone can see the main characteristics of Shakespeare's Comedies. They deal with the question of how to live, and particularly of how to treat other people in our varying relationships with them, from business to courtship. They tell of love and harmony, initially disturbed, finally restored. They contain low-life comedy, which always has an English flavour no matter in what country the main action is sited … In Shakespearean comedy the setting is fantastic, but the characters are credible.

To state the very obvious, plays are experiences in language and it goes without saying that this experience in Shakespeare is always a rich and rewarding one. In *Twelfth Night* there is wonderful poetry – even the parodic languages of the play's egotists have a kind of magnificence and the language used by the agents of misrule provides a lively colloquial colourfulness. Of Malvolio, Dover Wilson says:

in Shakespeare's hands his dream blossoms into a monstrous beauty, expressed in the magnificent magniloquence of post-Falstaffian prose, a beauty that rivals in its fashion that of Shylock's rhetoric or even Falstaff himself. As with Shylock, so with Malvolio: Shakespeare let himself go.

The play's opening lines are known by people who do not know the play itself and are taken by them – regardless of context, in which they are deployed as critical of the speaker – to express a kind of universal yearning.

As there is a close relationship between comedy and topicality, we have to work at understanding allusions that have folded back into time past – which not only means being prepared to grapple with footnote references to things no longer having meaning outside the play and with inevitable changes in language usage, but also with ways of thinking quite different to our own. "This is a practice/As full of labour as a wise man's art."

1

But That's All One

There are certain givens requiring us to exercise Coleridge's willing suspension of disbelief. Perhaps the most important among them is one from which nowadays we derive little benefit and because of which modern performances miss out on a particular dimension – though unisex productions can go some way towards. Namely, that in Shakespeare's theatre the women's parts were played by boys. Olivia, a countess, was played by a boy; Cesario, a gentlewoman by a boy, disguising 'herself' as a young man. Three layers of 'reality' are played out in her: a boy playing a woman disguised as a boy wooing a woman played by a boy. This extra dimension also allows for a variety of in-jokes. The fact that actors were referred to as 'shadows' and 'ciphers' adds yet another layer to the game of appearances *Twelfth Night* so nimbly plays.

Another is to do with location. Shakespeare alters the setting in his immediate source (Barnaby Rich's *Of Apolonius and Silla* in his *Farewell to a Military Profession*, 1581[1]) to an Illyria which is in effect as imaginary as *The Winter's Tale*'s Bohemia or Prospero's island in *The Tempest*, and only incidentally sharing a name with a region bordering the eastern Adriatic. Then there's the hotchpotch of the characters' names. In this imaginary Illyria are to be found the separate houses of aristocrats with foreign-sounding names (Orsino, Olivia) among relatives and hangers-on with English-sounding ones (Belch, Aguecheek), where Viola becomes Cesario, a Curio works alongside a Valentine, where there's an inn called *The Elephant*, and where a woman, strangely mourning the demise of a brother (but not of the father whose death predated the brother's by a month) has abjured the sight and company of men and yet has at least five of them (Sir Toby, Sir Andrew, Malvolio, Fabian and Feste – unless we

1

take it she means to abjure the sight and company only of potential wooers) in her house. An inescapable irony, however, is that Toby is offering to act as go-between on behalf of Aguecheek and that Malvolio thinks *he* has expectations. The names Sir Toby Belch and Sir Andrew Aguecheek are, as in Dickens or cartoons, simple and obvious determinants of character – as is the Italianate-sounding (but very English) steward, Malvolio, whose name, indicative of ill-will, could readily be applied to a malcontent in a Jacobean tragedy. Feste, suggestive of revels, becomes the ridiculous Sir Topas out of Chaucer. There even seems to be a slithery sort of punning going on with Viola, Olivia, Malvolio and M.O.A.I. – not to mention the references to an olive branch (Viola's "I hold the olive in my hand. My words are as full of peace as matter") and a viol-de-gamboys.

Among other givens are Feste's freedom – though officially attached to Olivia's household as her allowed fool – to travel between her house and Orsino's – as if somehow belonging to his court too – in order to fulfil the function in both places of earning a living by entertaining with his dexterous wit or feeding melancholy with sad songs. He himself explains it simply: "Foolery, sir, does walk about the orb like the sun; it shines everywhere." And we have to accept that, though he has licence to say almost anything to his betters and get away with it (his truths can always be laughed away), he can, for being absent or late, be punished severely. At the beginning of Act I, scene 5, we find Maria scolding him thus:

> Nay, either tell me where thou hast been, or I will
> not open my lips so wide as a bristle may enter, in way of
> thy excuse. My lady will hang thee for thy absence.

A professional fool – and this is confirmed in other plays – knows he is engaged in a very risky business. Hanging or whipping is part of the job description. There is a dangerous connection between wordplay and responsibility – which will be looked at in some detail later. And this leads to the general observation, often made, that the comedy of love is never far removed from danger: jesters' lives can be threatened; characters emerge from a shipwreck; fathers and brothers die; Antonio, at risk on enemy territory, is arrested; there are challenges to duels and broken pates; dukedoms and noble households are subject to misrule; Malvolio is "notoriously abused";

and the whirligig of time threatens to bring in its revenges.

Then there's the convention (the 'wickedness') of twin-gender-swapping (not easy to get away with in the theatre without a willing suspension of disbelief or generosity on the part of the audience, or a director interprets it as a gay play) made more complicated by what we said above about boy actors and disguise. And we are obliged unquestioningly to accept the business in the last scene of Viola and Sebastian fortuitously appearing in identical costumes. We are required to forget, as Shakespeare seems to have done, the fact that Viola suggests disguising herself as "an eunuch" (unless we take this to suggest the kind of voice she will put on) and the captain's wish to accompany her as a "mute". And then there's forging someone else's handwriting. Not forgetting the part played by coincidence in the action nor the way characters have, in their speeches, of being articulate about their condition. There is always ambivalence about this. Is it part of their condition – their suffering for instance – that they are conscious of things wrong about themselves and at the same time conscious of being unable to undo them? Or is it simply Shakespeare forwarding the plot?

Finally there is the question of Act-division, which Harley Granville-Barker, at the beginning of the last century, was among the first to draw attention to. There is something to be said for his argument. Of *Twelfth Night* he says this:

> I am pretty sure that Shakespeare's performance went through without a break. Certainly its conventional arrangement into five acts for the printing of the Folio is neither by Shakespeare nor any sensitive hand; it is shockingly bad. If one must have intervals (as the discomforts of most theatres demand), I think the play falls as easily into the three divisions I have marked as any (i.e. after II.iii and IV.i).

Needless to say, little of the above gives trouble during performance … unless of course the production is a poor one.

Notes

[1] For a useful account of how Shakespeare adapted his main source see the Introduction to *Elizabethan Love Stories*, ed. T.J.B. Spencer, Penguin Shakespeare Library, 1968.

2

What Is Love?

Feste's answer to his own question is "not hereafter". Love is to be experienced in the lived-in present. "Present mirth hath present laughter". You don't get anywhere by hanging about. Desist from 'roaming', stick around, and listen to what your true love has to say. It is the standard *carpe diem* theme of much love poetry, going back at least to the Latin poet, Ovid: the message is: get it while you can, "Youth's the stuff will not endure". Feste's song is a concise expression of the theme of mutability extensively found in the poetry of the period – an obsession with the passing of time (the "wingèd chariot" of Marvell who tells his mistress that coyness – "Had we but world enough and time" – is all very well but ...) The result is a sharpened sensitivity, born of the knowledge that nothing lasts and "our little life is rounded with a sleep".

Feste's song provides us with the plot in miniature: the journey the play undertakes does end in lovers meeting and in the realisation of what "Every wise man's son doth know", namely that "In delay there lies no plenty." As Marvell wooingly puts it:

> Now therefore, while the youthful hue
> Sits on thy skin like morning dew,
> And while thy willing soul transpires
> At every pore with instant fires,
> Now let us sport us while we may,
> And now, like amorous birds of prey,
> Rather at once our time devour
> Than languish in his slow-chapped power.

It is in the tradition of Petrarchan love poetry that lovers languish and complain, as in "Come away, come away, death." "O mistress

4

mine" offers a corrective and is acutely anti-Petrarchan.

And yet Feste – and this is both the curse and the gift of Shakespearean clowns – is the only character in the play – until the ending that is – with this realisation to hand; he is ironically the one person in the play without expectations, other than the monetary hand-outs he has to survive on. Others (Orsino, Olivia) have to be brought to it through complication, coincidence, the untying of the "too hard a knot" Cesario speaks of at the end of Act II, scene 2. The audience, though conscious from the start that a happy ending is on the cards, is encouraged to keep asking "How will this fadge?" (turn out) – concerned not so much with satisfactory outcomes as with the wittily-created processes by which they may be achieved.

Orsino is in love with love or, rather, involved in the fashionable cult-idea of it, fed by Petrarchan poetry. "He has," says Dover Wilson:

> steeped himself, we may imagine, in Petrarch; he prefers worshipping at a distance, and wooing by proxy; he likes to stab himself with the thought of the cruelty of his adored.

It is a form of melancholy (from which Olivia also suffers). Middleton Murry, seeing the play as "sad, partly with the weight of its own beauty, but sad also with a wistfulness to which Shakespeare could not help giving direct expression", finds something deeper, going as far as to suggest it's

> not the perfunctory and conventional lover's melancholy, of which Shakespeare had so often and so happily made fun. It is the Melancholy of Keats' ode, the sovereign goddess who
>
> *Dwells with beauty, beauty that must die*
> And joy whose hand is ever at his lips
> Bidding adieu.

Well, maybe. Orsino is, despite himself, mad with the idea of love, suffering from idle melancholy – which Robert Burton in his great exploration of the subject, *The Anatomy of Melancholy* (1621), sees as an "inbred malady in all of us" (note the connection with ill-health) – a form of mental illness, but one that can be recovered from. "Be not solitary, be not idle," Burton advises. The Duke is a would-be melancholic, a man divided against himself, as is evident in two kinds of language we hear him speak.

Orsino has set Olivia up as an object, an icon, of adoration – safely at a distance – simply because she purports to be unavailable. In other words he is playing the game of courtly love, in which the beloved is put on a pedestal, seen as unattainable and worshipped from afar. It is chivalric: the lover, suffering for love, is in the process ennobled. *Princeton Encyclopedia of Poetry and Poetics* has this to tell us:

> Courtly Love is a noble passion; the courtly lover idealizes his beloved; she, his sovereign lady, occupies an exalted position over him; his feelings for her ennoble him and make him more worthy; her beauty of body and soul makes him long for union with her, not for passion's sake but as a means of achieving the ultimate in moral excellence.

J. Denomy, quoted in the above, adds the following features sometimes found in courtly lovers:

> the personification of love as a god with absolute power over his army of lovers, the idea of love as a sickness with all its familiar exterior manifestations, the ceaseless fears of the lover at losing his beloved, at displeasing her, the position of inferiority of the lover and the feeling of timidity to which the feeling gives rise, the capriciousness, haughtiness and disdain of the beloved, the need for secrecy, stealth and furtiveness in the intrigue, the danger of tale-bearers, and so on.

The business is ritualistic, a sort of secular religion (it has parallels with the medieval cult of the Virgin Mary); it is serious in intent, its aim being that of aspiring to virtue. What Shakespeare is pointing to is the distance between aspiration or ambition and actual fulfilment.

With Orsino the intent is – at least in his mind – serious, but he has allowed himself to become the victim of fashionable posturing – to the point of masochistic self-indulgence, paralleling the self-love Malvolio is accused of and caught out in. (*Twelfth Night* is built up of a series of parallels and contrasts as we are perhaps already beginning to see).

Orsino is languishing in what Julia in *Brideshead Revisited* calls "an amorous stupor", his melancholy fed by lugubrious music, his thoughts obsessed with Love – and not, we may note, on ducal responsibilities. It is not unusual for productions nowadays to portray him as one of the idle rich. Shakespeare has fun with Orsino's language, playing with the connections between music, love, food, illness, sweet-smelling flowers, excess … and dying. Lovers often wish for death or accuse their disdainful mistress of slaying them, as in Feste's second song in Act II, scene 4 – and Shakespeare's audience would not fail to pick up on the sexual meanings in this of experiencing the 'little death' of orgasm. Eating, too, has sexual overtones – there is a traditional connection between lust and gluttony – providing a strong source of imagery for it. Lechery says in Marlowe's *Doctor Faustus*: "I am one who loves an inch of raw mutton better than an ell of fried stockfish."

Orsino wants to indulge the senses, to gorge himself to death, to overwhelm himself and his attendants with impressive noble sentiments, a feast of grand-sounding clichés derived from courtly love poetry, or to use a metaphor more in keeping with the themes and motifs of the play, he is drunk with words:

> O spirit of love, how quick and fresh art thou,
> That, notwithstanding thy capacity
> Receiveth as the sea, naught enters there,
> Of what validity and pitch soe'er,
> But falls into abatement and low price
> Even in a minute. So full of shapes is fancy
> That it alone is high fantastical.
>
> (Act I, scene 1, 9-15)

What true lovers really demonstrate is constancy. Shakespeare's sonnet 116 puts this very clearly:

> Let me not to the marriage of true minds
> Admit impediments; love is not love
> Which alters when it alteration finds,
> Nor bends with the remover to remove:
> O, no, it is an ever fixèd mark,
> That looks on tempests and is never shaken;
> It is the star to every wandering bark,
> Whose worth's unknown, although his highth be taken.

Love's not Time's foole, though rosy lips and cheeks
Within his bending sickle's compass come;
Love alters not with his brief hours and weeks,
But bears it out even to the edge of doom.
    If this be error and upon me proved,
    I never writ, nor no man ever loved.

Helena tells us in *A Midsummer Night's Dream*, that "Love looks not with the eyes, but with the mind". The song in *The Merchant of Venice*, 'Where is Fancy bred', answers its own question by saying "It is engend'red in the eyes,/With gazing fed". And there's the rub. This business of "with the mind" is an ideal that lovers, in the first flush of attachment, hardly ever live up to; they usually see what they want to see. Othello and Desdemona are as guilty as any in this, deceiving themselves into thinking that theirs is a marriage of true minds. Think of Titania looking with love at Bottom in the guise of an ass. In romantic comedy, love has the habit of too readily entering in at the eye. The effects are comic: they lead to false conclusions and confusion. Love is regarded as an infection, a kind of madness, a sort of moral drunkenness, in which inconstancy is its prominent feature. Orsino asks for music then suddenly orders "Enough, no more!" Inconstancy promotes unpredictability. "How will this fadge?" we keep asking.

For the moment let's note that Orsino's language indicates a divided self: it is overblown, poetic in a bad sense (in the final scene he can still talk this way; he exclaims "Here comes the Countess; now heaven walks on earth"[1]); it points to a moral and emotional instability, a self-love as unhealthy as Malvolio's. And when we hear him earlier in Act II we might even ask if there is something misogynistic in his:

There is no woman's sides
Can bide the beating of so strong a passion
As love doth give my heart; no woman's heart
So big to hold so much, they lack retention.
Alas, their love may be called appetite,
No motion of the liver, but the palate,
That suffer surfeit, cloyment, and revolt.
But mine is all as hungry as the sea,

And can digest as much. Make no compare
Between that love a woman can bear me
And that I owe Olivia.

(Act II, scene 4, 93-102)

This is an extraordinary piece of arrogance, a pompous statement of male superiority. It is not Olivia he loves but himself ennobled by a passion "as hungry as the sea". The logic of what he says is that no woman can match his passion and therefore is unworthy of it. It is not a marriage of true minds he is seeking. The very qualities he despises in women ("their love may be called appetite") are manifest in him. One cannot ignore the sexual pressure in his words. One may even consider it masturbatory. How can he dare to condemn women for "surfeit, cloyment" when these are such features of his own behaviour? And in his word "revolt" meaning 'revulsion' isn't there something anti-sex as well as anti-women? And yet there is something contradictory in his pronouncement:

Let still the woman take
An elder than herself; so wears she to him;
So sways she level in her husband's heart.
For, boy, however we do praise ourselves,
Our fancies are more giddy and unfirm,
More longing, wavering, sooner lost and worn,
Than women's are.

(Act II, scene 4, 29-35)

an example perhaps of inconstancy, unless (and this is persuasive) his more rational self is here speaking not in the clichés but with a truer voice, with the sanity born of experience, perhaps allowing us to understand what Viola has seen in him, what has made *her* fall in love. All this is conjecture; it is just as possible that she is as deluded as he is. It is the above speech that tempts biographers to make connections with Shakespeare's marriage to the older Anne Hathaway. So too the reference to "Arion on the dolphins's back" in Act I, scene 2, seduces them into wanting to ask "Did alderman John Shakespeare, the Stratford Glover, take his eleven-year-old son to glimpse the Queen and share her wonder at the entertainments the Earl of Leicester put on for her at his castle at Kenilworth in 1575?"[2]

In the scene (Act III, scene 1) in which Viola/Cesario has a contest

9

of wits with Feste and in which the ways that language can be corrupted are discussed, Viola makes the statement: "They that dally nicely with words may quickly make them wanton". This applies to virtually every character in the play. (The word "wanton" has sexual overtones). In Orsino's case, one only has to judge his reaction to Curio's suggestion that they go out hunting: he deliberately pounces on the word "hart" (with its unspoken pun on 'heart') in order to turn himself into Acteon who, as a punishment for catching sight of the goddess, Diana, nakedly bathing, had his hounds directed against him and, while retaining his human consciousness, was ripped to pieces. In other words, he hears only what he wants to hear and what suits his prevailing mood, the noble lover complaining of his mistress's cruelty and self-indulgently relishing his victimhood. It is not without irony that the business of making contact with Olivia is done by intermediaries, go-betweens, while Orsino stays home in the luxury of languor among his servants. The society which the play presents to us is, of course, hierarchical: the relationship between servants and their so-called betters is at its heart. Valentine, who is soon to be replaced in the office of go-between by Cesario, has spoken with Olivia's lady-in-waiting, Maria, and not with the disdainful lady herself. Note that not taking no for an answer is part of the amatory game. All of the above, and more, is being signalled in the play's first five minutes.

Notes

[1] Compare this with Sonnet 130 in which Shakespeare writes:
> *I graunt I never saw a goddesse goe,*
> *My mistres when shee walks treads on the ground*

[2] See for example *William Shakespeare His Life and Work* by Anthony Holden, (Abacus, 1999) and *Will in the World* by Stephen Greenblatt, (Jonathan Cape, 2004).

3

Like a Cloistress

Love takes on various guises in the play, some giving meaning for us by running parallel to others, some working by contrast. Love of any god other than the god of love is, to all intents and purposes, omitted ... though it is impossible to ignore the place of devil in it as a deceiver and an abuser of men's wits. Love between master and mistress (Viola will become "Orsino's mistress and his fancy's queen"), between brothers and sisters (parents are notably absent from this play), and between friends and companions (Sebastian and Antonio, Viola and the Captain). But the main target of the play is life-impairing self-love. There is the transgressive love of Malvolio for his countess-employer and her 'forged' (declared in Maria's letter) love for him. Requited love (Sir Toby and Maria), and unrequited love. And there's once-upon-a-time love: perhaps the most poignant line in all Shakespeare is Sir Andrew's "I was adored once too". A running contrast between real and mistaken love energises the whole play. Eventually, there is married love, which aspires to the condition of constancy, to a marriage of true minds. And there is love of things – cakes and ale, dancing and singing, exchanges of wit – and, above all, love of life itself.

Olivia has decided on a grossly excessive period of mourning for a brother. Not even royalty claims more than a year – a fact of significance to a reading of *Hamlet*, written possibly the year after. Olivia's decision to play the cloistress (her seal, as Dover Wilson points out "is an intaglio of Lucrece, the classical type of chastity") and abjure the sight and company of men for seven years, is made to sound even more perverse in view of the fact, mentioned earlier, that though her "sad remembrance" is for a "brother's dead love" (rather than a dead brother?) it is not for the father dying a month earlier that she turns herself into a secular nun. (Note that she wears the veil in her first interview with Cesario.) It is interesting to note, in passing, that Viola and Sebastian have no trouble remembering the fact that their father had died thirteen years previously.

There is a kind of Alice-in-Wonderland absurdity in the report Olivia will:

> ... water once a day her chamber round
> With eye-offending brine;
>
> (Act I scene 1, 30-1)

What kind of cloistress? Her uncle Toby asks "What a plague means my niece to take the death of her brother thus? I am sure care's an enemy to life", and her handmaid, Maria, makes no bones about it either, describing her mistress as being "addicted to melancholy". We soon discover that her household is actually peopled with men – among them Sir Andrew, a would-be wooer; and soon recognise it as a place of ungoverned bad behaviour, a house of misrule. As with Orsino, there is hypocrisy at work. Appearance and reality are in conflict; self-indulgence and responsibility are being set up again for judgement.

Of course, nothing is as clear-cut as this seems. I don't want to sound like Malvolio. There are ambivalences at work. Since (for the most part) we expect happy outcomes, part of us envies the freedoms allowed to the various characters; to varying degrees we sympathise with them in their predicaments; and part of us has at least a sneaking regard for the pleasures of excess (Blake said "The road of excess leads to the palace of wisdom" and asked "How do you know what is enough until you know what is more than enough?") This now perhaps makes clear the connection with the celebration of Twelfth Night, the final evening of the Christmas season, a twelve-day period of licence, of letting off steam, the world turned topsy-turvy for a limited space. In England a

> Twelfth Night cake is usually a rich dense fruitcake which contains both a bean and a pea. The man who finds the bean is the King, the woman who finds the pea is the queen. But, if the woman finds the bean, she can choose the King, while the man who finds the pea can choose the Queen. The royal pair

> then direct the rest of the company in merriment. They assign
> ludicrous tasks or require them to behave in ways contrary to
> their usual roles … Traditional foods served in England include
> anything spicy or hot, like ginger snaps and spiced ale.

In other words, for a specifically designated time, we, the audience, can claim the privileges of a licensed fool. (In the light of the reference at the end of the above, we may find ourselves reminded of Sir Toby's famous question flung at Malvolio "Dost thou think, because thou art virtuous, there shall be no more cakes and ale?" and Feste's rider "Yes, by Saint Anne, and ginger shall be hot I' th' mouth too.")

Twelfth Night is not a Jonsonian comedy. As Hazlitt says:

> It makes us laugh at the follies of mankind, not despise them,
> and still less bear any ill-will towards them … Much as we
> like catches and cakes and ale, there is something we like
> better. We have a friendship for Sir Toby; we patronise Sir
> Andrew; we have an understanding with the Clown, a sneaking
> kindness for Maria and her rogueries; we feel a regard for
> Malvolio, and sympathise with his gravity, his smiles, his cross
> garters, his yellow stockings, and his imprisonment in the
> stocks. But there is something that excites in us stronger feeling
> than all this – it is Viola's confession of her love.

This is perhaps running ahead a little. What I want to emphasise is that Shakespeare's main wish is to ensure that what we witness "May rather pluck on laughter than revenge,/If that the injuries be justly weighed." But again this is not clear cut, since *Twelfth Night* juggles with our sense of justice (as it may be in the real world) and with poetic justice, the whirligig of time bringing in its revenges. For the moment let's pose the intriguing question: how easy would it be to imagine a sequel entitled *Malvolio's Revenge*?

Both Orsino and Olivia purport to cut themselves off from life, both act in a quasi-religious way, one devoted to the adoration of an icon, the other to an unduly long period of sad remembrance (she has built a chapel dedicated to her brother's memory); both enjoy bouts of melancholy. I say purport simply to re-emphasise the conflict between what people aspire to and what they actually do or achieve. In tragedies this conflict leads to fatal consequences; in comedies life itself – in the form of fate, time, events, coincidences, what you will – intervenes, stirs things up and finally sorts them all out. And, with fine irony, both Orsino and Olivia may be said to provoke and achieve the opposite effect from what they have intended.

Love with Orsino entered at the eye ("O, when mine eyes did see Olivia first"), though when and where are not explained; so too with Olivia – though she is shrewd enough to ask Cesario at their first meeting "What is your parentage?" Once the Duke's messenger has gone she considers:

> 'What is your parentage?'
> 'Above my fortunes, yet my state is well.
> I am a gentlemen.' I'll be sworn thou art.
> Thy tongue, thy face, thy limbs, actions, and spirit
> Do give thee fivefold blazon. Not too fast! soft, soft –
> Unless the master were the man. How now?
> Even so quickly may one catch the plague?
> Methinks I feel this youth's perfections,
> With an invisible and subtle stealth,
> To creep in at mine eyes.
>
> (Act I, scene 5, 278-87)

Her word "plague" echoes Orsino's "pestilence" in the first scene. Needless to say the threat of plague was no joke to Shakespeare and his audiences. Note that in the mouth of Toby the word "plague" is used as a curse.

Olivia's falling in love also betrays her into thinking with the clichés of courtly love and its language. She has been, as it were, mesmerised by the promise of "adorations … fertile tears … groans that thunder love … sighs of fire." (All of which tells us that Viola too is well-versed in the language of courtly love – though here using it deliberately, parodically. She is capable of two kinds of language, sometimes in the same speech – the language of feigning and the language that speaks truth). Later in the play Olivia confronts Cesario/Viola with the following:

> O, what a deal of scorn looks beautiful
> In the contempt and anger of his lip!
> A murderous guilt shows not itself more soon
> Than love that would seem hid; love's night is noon.

(*To Viola*) Cesario, by the roses of the spring,
By maidhood, honour, truth, and everything,
I love thee so that, maugre all thy pride,
Nor wit nor reason can my passion hide.
Do not extort thy reasons from this clause:
For that I woo, thou therefore hast no cause.
But rather reason thus with reason fetter:
Love sought, is good; but given unsought, is better.

(Act III, scene 1, 142-53)

This stretch of rhyming verse sounds almost like a failed sonnet
– sonnets being the favourite form for love poets. Love has turned
Olivia's world upside-down; night is confused with noon; and the
sovereign qualities of wit and reason have no power to hide what she
feels. She too experiences love as a delicious form of suffering. And
if Cesario has now exchanged roles with Feste (" … now I am your
fool"), then Olivia now occupies the same position as Orsino, both
of them suffering the pangs of despised love. There is pleasure for
us in this for what is clearly catcher-caught poetic justice. It makes a
nonsense of Olivia's vow to abjure the sight of men; yet it also primes
her for the appearance of Sebastian, to whom she gets betrothed in
the chantry built to honour the memory of her brother. In a nutshell,
she is beginning, despite her vow, to enter the real world.

4

One Heart, One Bosom, and One Truth

Both Orsino and Olivia are intent on performing quasi-religious rites involving withdrawal from the real world: it is as if each has joined a cult. And if their motives are, at least in their own eyes, honourable, the keynote is of things being taken to excess, a transgression of the Golden Mean, which would perhaps imply hidden motives, maybe distrust of life itself. Whether this be the case or not, life is not going to, and in the event, does not allow them to remain foolish overlong. They will at least both learn that "In delay there lies no plenty."

Life, on the other hand, takes Viola by the scruff of the neck. She is victim of a shipwreck, fortunate in that she survives, but landing in a strange country, vulnerable, a young woman separated from a twin brother and without his protection or means. It is a commonplace of commentaries on *Twelfth Night* to highlight – in contrast to the behaviour of Olivia and the Duke – Viola's resilience, her realism, her practical and positive nature. The poignant word-play of "Illyria"/ "Elysium" is an immediate demonstration that punning can be used to serious effect and indicate someone of real feelings. It is nothing like the tendentious reaction of Orsino to the word "hart" nor the irresponsible wordplay of Sir Toby or the feeble-minded confusions of Sir Andrew. It is more in keeping with the Clown's wisdom, his 'wit' – as demonstrated in Feste's catechising of Olivia:

> FESTE Good madonna, why mourn'st thou?
> OLIVIA Good fool, for my brother's death.
> FESTE I think his soul is in hell, madonna.
> OLIVIA I know his soul is in heaven, fool.
> FESTE The more fool, madonna, to mourn for your
>   brother's soul, being in heaven.

(Act I, scene 5, 61-6)

Here Olivia loses out in the game of wits: the *mad*-onna is shown to be mad in her denial of reality. In contrast, Viola gives more or less as good as she gets with Feste.

Viola's first thoughts after wishing to know where fate has cast her up are less for herself than for her brother. The keynotes in her conversation with the Captain are altruism and belief in Providence. We hear the word "perchance" three times in quick succession, soon followed by the word "chance" itself, and then the word "provident". She does not view her situation as an occasion for melancholy. The emphasis is on hope and faith:

> Mine own escape unfoldeth to my hope,
> Whereto thy speech serves for authority,
> The like of him.
>
> (Act I, scene 2, 19-21)

This hope is something she hangs on to and something that is tested in the play. In Act II, scene 4, 119-20, she states: "I am all the daughters of my father's house,/And all the brothers too; and yet,/I know not …" This last sentiment leaves open the possibility that Sebastian has been as fortunate as she. And she rewards the Captain ("For saying so, there's gold"), the sure sign in Shakespeare of a virtuous character, someone who recognises virtue and worth in others. Now, having escaped drowning, she must find a form of protection, a way of allowing life to continue for her. Her survival has given her what amounts to a realisation of the preciousness of life, heightened for her by the hope of her brother's survival. Contrast with Orsino and with Olivia has been quickly determined and the play is only minutes old.

At this point it might help if we pause to think of the general attitudes to women the play seems to assume. Orsino is in no doubt: "Women are as roses whose fair flower,/Being once displayed, doth fall that very hour." He is only interested in woman as image, icon. There is, as we have noted, something at the same time misogynistic in his speech in Act II, scene 4 in which he haughtily compares the fullness of his affections to what a woman is capable of feeling. Odious arrogance aside, his 'logic' betrays a mind with small semblance of reason. If women are so grossly inferior why choose one to be the object of one's love? They are obviously unworthy of such passion! That is the logic of it. Viola/Cesario's answer to this is that women (feeling but unable to show her love) are "as true of heart" as men. And yet she too expresses the conventional view of Shakespeare's time when she says:

> How easy is it for the proper false
> In women's waxen hearts to set their forms.
> Alas, our frailty is the cause, not we,
> For such as we are made, if such we be.
>
> (Act II, scene 2, 29-32)

Perhaps what we are meant to recognise here though is her common-sense practical acceptance of her lot.

The play balances a male and a female in authority, a Countess and a Duke, neither having full control of their situations. And if the play does suggest that women are or perceive themselves to be more vulnerable (Viola's need to disguise herself as a man is evidence), it also shows that women do most of the controlling and in many ways are more forceful than the male characters. Practical and resilient, Viola maintains "One heart, one bosom, and one truth". Maria too is a force to reckon with: it looks as though she runs the affairs of Olivia's household more capably (can we say more even-handedly?) than either her melancholy-infected mistress or her steward, Malvolio.

The perspective from which we judge all these matters is the ideal contained in the phrase a "marriage of true minds".

5

Give Me Some Music

Take but degree away, untune that string,
And hark what discord follows.
(Troilus and Cressida, Act I, scene 3, 109-10)

Music – singing and dancing to it – has an active role to play in
Twelfth Night. The play opens and closes with music. Orsino bathes
in it emotionally; Sir Toby and Sir Andrew cut capers to it and, along
with Feste, boisterously sing catches; Sir Andrew is said to play the
viol-de-gamboys; and singing is part of Feste's stock in trade,
something he is paid to do. We have courtly songs, popular songs,
folk songs, as well as whatever incidental music might be played.
That Shakespeare's company had in 1599 acquired the services of
Robert Armin – so different from his knockabout predecessor, Will
Kemp – had a clear effect upon the writing of the play. Armin was a
more sophisticated clown than Kemp and an accomplished singer.

Music was part of a genteel education. Castiglione's highly
influential book, *Il Cortegiano*, (*The Courtier*), was translated by
Thomas Hoby in 1561. According to the well-known writer on music,
Eric Blom, Castilglione's recommendations were readily taken to
heart by courtiers and gentlemen because they "included suggestions
which at once flattered their vanity and encouraged dilettantish
indolence". (He might be talking of Orsino – though the Duke is no
performer himself: music for him, like his love life, offers vicarious
experience). Blom quotes the following passage:

> I would not our courtier should doe as many doe, that as soone
> as they come into any place, and also in the presence of great
> men with whome they have no acquaintance at all, without
> much entreating set out them selves, to shew as much as they

know, yea and many times that they know not, so that a man would weene they came purposely to shew themselves for that, and that is their principall profession.

Therefore let our Courtier come to showe his musick as a thing to passe the time withal, and as he were enforced to doe it, and not in the presence of noble men, nor of any great multitude.

And for he be skilfull and doth well understand it, yet will I have him to dissemble the studie and paines that a man needs take in all things that are well done. And let him make semblance that he esteemeth but little of him selfe that qualitie, but in doing it excellently well, make it much esteemed of other men.

Theories of music, going back to Pythagoras, were based upon the idea of celestial harmonies; earthly music was thought to emulate the "angelic symphony" of heavenly music. So too, in its rhythmical patternings, dance was a way of emulating divinely ordained order. As Sir John Davies in his poem 'Orchestra', published in 1596, says:

Kind nature first doth cause all things to love;
Love makes them dance and in just order move.

The effect, if not the purpose, of comedy is to bring order out of chaos, concord out of discord, to put value on constancy. (Shakespeare has much to say about music and its power, about "concord of sweet sounds" and how "sour sweet music is/When time is broke, and not proportion kept").[1] *Twelfth Night* explores various kinds of disorder: mental (who escapes the charge of being mad?); social (drunken revels, staying up "betimes", the "uncivil rule" Maria accuses the revellers of); infected wits caused by falling in love; irresponsibility (the Duke tells Cesario, in his embassy to Olivia, to "Be clamorous and leap all civil bounds/Rather than make unprofited return."); the excesses of mourning allowing disorderliness to thrive; and linguistic disorder, corruption of language.

Drowning and escape from it are also motifs in the play: one may drown in water, in tears, in madness, in drink.

OLIVIA What's a drunken man like, fool?

FESTE Like a drowned man, a fool, and a madman. One
    draught above heat makes him a fool, the second mads
    him, and a third drowns him.

OLIVIA Go thou and see the crowner, and let him sit o'
    my coz, for he's in the third degree of drink – he's
    drowned.

(Act I, scene 5, 125-31)

When the play opens Orsino is drowning in music, indulging his melancholy in a combination of arrogance and self-pity. The music has 'a dying fall' (cadence). His reactions to it are fickle: in his "Enough, no more!" he demonstrates a failure of constancy and his distractedness.

In a sense, Viola becomes Orsino's allowed fool. Telling the Captain she will disguise herself as "an eunuch", she declares, as Armin would have been able to say:

> … for I can sing
> And speak to him in many sorts of music
> That will allow me very worth his service.

(Act I, scene 2, 58-60)

Olivia's disorderly household is the scene of drunken revels: viols, catches, galliards and cutting capers. Music here is to be viewed as a failed attempt at, or even a gross parody of, harmony. It is rather to use Maria's word, mere "caterwauling" and earns Malvolio's rebuke: "Do ye make an alehouse of my lady's house, that ye squeak out your coziers' catches without any mitigation or remorse of voice? Is there no respect of place, person, nor time in you?", only for him to earn the riposte: "We did keep time, sir, in our catches. Sneck up!" – in other words, go hang yourself. In this scene (Act II, scene 3) Feste has only five minutes previously sung the beautiful anti-Petrarchan "O mistress mine", which may be said to contain the play's essential wisdoms.

When we meet the Duke again in Act II, we hear him requesting "That old and antic song we heard last night" and self-importantly criticising the "light airs and recollected terms/Of these most brisk and giddy-pacèd times." Viola, when asked "How dost thou like this tune?" replies:

21

It gives a very echo to the seat
Where love is throned.

(Act II scene 4, 21-2)

This is either her indulging her master in his taste for melancholy or an admission of her own frustrated feelings of love. When Feste sings for the Duke, the song seems to be anti-life: in it the wretched lover, in an ambivalence of self-pity and chivalric ennoblement, mourns his own death, slain by a "fair cruel maid" (the "sovereign cruelty", Olivia).[2] It is no surprise that Feste remarks disparagingly afterwards: "Now the melancholy god protect thee, and the tailor make thy doublet of changeable taffeta, for thy mind is a very opal. I would have men of such constancy put to sea, that their business might be everything, and their intent everywhere; for that's it that always makes a good voyage of nothing."

At the end of Act IV, scene 2, Feste, having cast off the Sir Topas disguise, promises to aid Malvolio by bringing paper and ink, and goes off singing: the burden of his song, being one of Christian compassion, implies a promise to help Malvolio resist the wiles of the devil (who is, as we have noted, present in various guises in the play).

For the moment we will leave the song Feste sings at the end – only make the obvious observation that after sunshine comes the rain.

Notes

[1] See Lorenzo in *The Merchant of Venice*, Act V, scene 1, and Richard's prison soliloquy in *Richard II,* Act V, scene 5.

[2] There is a temptation to read the line 'In sad cypress let me be laid' as a wish to be buried in a grove of cypresses. It may also mean in a coffin made of cypress wood or a kind of fabric associated with mourning.

6

To Time I Will Commit

In music you are meant to keep time (remember Toby's "We did keep time, sir, in our catches"). It is not without significance that a word like 'divisions' is used to describe musical structures or that the word 'measures' means dance-steps. Courtly dancing is not an inapposite metaphor for a comedy like *Twelfth Night* – the play is like a courtly dance in which the dancers haven't mastered the steps or have forgotten them or egotistically want to dominate or keep falling over drunkenly. In the end they honour their partners, become capable of making proper patterns, and are ready to be in tune with the world. Except those, of course, who will not join the dance or who are congenitally incapable of mastering the steps. And it is not for nothing that groups of musicians are called consorts, their aim in playing being to achieve a 'concord of sweet sounds.'

Human beings live in the world of time, their lives subject to change and decay, and are engaged in the process which Eliot calls "birth, copulation, and death". Comedy, on the side of life, therefore sees as foolish the waste of precious time in its characters. The message to Orsino and Olivia is "Youth's a stuff will not endure."

Consciousness of living in the world of time implies and assumes a consciousness of another context – namely eternity, timelessness, where nothing suffers change, the dimension inhabited by God and his angels. It is in this dimension that divine harmonies, of which earthly musics and the ideal of living in harmony, as we have already indicated, can only afford a taste, exist. Hence the carpe diem theme of love poetry: the urgency of getting it together. Song and dance are communal activities which draw people together into orderly patterns of behaviour; they correspond to law and order in the state. It has long been a commonplace of Shakespearean criticism that his plays are explorations of the themes of order and disorder.

What of time then in *Twelfth Night*? Olivia's decision to mourn her brother's death for seven years is an aunt-sally quickly knocked down after a year's observance (the captain tells Viola that Olivia's a "virtuous maid, the daughter of a count/That died some twelvemonth since"). We meet the denizens of her household before we meet her: Toby and Aguecheek (who, debauched as they are, have noble status and pretensions) are abusers of time, as well as drink and the peace:

> MARIA By my troth, Sir Toby, you must come in earlier
>   o'nights. Your cousin, my lady, takes great exceptions to
>   your ill hours.
> SIR TOBY Why, let her except before excepted.
> MARIA Ay, but you must confine yourself within the
>   modest limits of order.
>
>   (Act I, scene 3, 3-8)

The phrase "disorderly hours" is appropriate here. Maria's advice (namely to "confine yourself within the modest limits of order", central to the play's concerns) is ignored, as we see a little further on in Act II, scene 3, in which Sir Toby uses false logic to licence deviant behaviour:

> SIR TOBY Approach, Sir Andrew. Not to be abed after
>   midnight, is to be up betimes, and *dilucolo surgere*,
>   thou knowest –
> SIR ANDREW Nay, by my troth, I know not; but I know
>   to be up late is to be up late.
> SIR TOBY A false conclusion! I hate it as an unfilled can.
>   To be up after midnight and to go to bed then is early;
>   so that to go to bed after midnight is to go to bed be-
>   times.
>
>   (Act II, scene 3, 1-9)

On the face of it, this is mere quibbling self-justification. But in case anyone thinks I sound like Malvolio, let me say that, like everyone else, I hope I am appreciative of the humour at work here and to a degree vicariously admire – as we are all meant to – the sentiments, securely within the imaginary space of the play, of those who take unashamed liberties. The final laugh is that the time taken up by the scene gives Toby the perfect excuse: "'Tis too late to go to bed now." Olivia's statement that "love's night is noon" with her is of a piece with Toby and Andrew's subversion of time, as is Toby's easily persuading Sir Andrew to go back on his decision to "not stay a jot longer" in Act III, scene 2.

But time has another role. *Twelfth Night* is a play in which no on-stage supernatural agencies – like Oberon and Puck with their spells in *A Midsummer Night's Dream* or Prospero with his magic books and Ariel in *The Tempest* – are pulling the strings. That is unless we equate Chance-Fate-Time with Providence (God's intentions for the world) as being active. Hamlet tells us there "is providence in the fall of a sparrow": in other words, everything that happens is God's will.

God – in this play often given the name Jove (Malvolio for example thanks Jove in Act II, scene 4 and again in Act III, scene 4 for what he believes is his good fortune) – is not much mentioned in *Twelfth Night*, though, as we stated earlier, his counterpart, the devil, is frequently referred to, cropping up in a variety of guises (for example in Act II, Viola declares "Disguise, I see thou art a wicked-ness/Wherein the pregnant enemy does much") in order to deceive, drive mad, betray into behaving like a beast. (In *Othello* Cassio gives us this meaningful equation when he describes the effects of drink: "To be now a man, by and by a fool, and presently a beast"; he also refers to the "devil drunkenness". Think of Bottom the Weaver in *A Midsummer Night's Dream* 'translated' into an ass). It is the devil's work to take the man, madden him, and make him behave bestially.

It is clear that in comedy, Chance-Fate-Time is given a free hand, whereas in tragedy events are to a large extent character-driven (consequences tending to arise from fatal choices). We have already noticed how Viola, thinking of her brother's possible fate, holds on to "perchance he is not drowned" and the Captain describes Sebastian as being "Most provident in peril". This trust (belief in Providence, an affirmation of Christian faith) seems to provide her with a necessary courage and hope (the Captain ascribes these qualities to her seemingly-lost brother and the fact that they are twins strongly suggests she will share them) to move virtuously – though not fearlessly – through the events of the play. It enables her to state, on deciding to become Cesario and serve the Duke, "What else may hap, I will to time commit" and later, discovering that Olivia has fallen for her in her man's guise:

> O time, thou must untangle this, not I!
> It is too hard a knot for me t'untie.
>
> (Act II, scene 2, 40-1)

Then again, when Malvolio catches up with her and throws the ring at her feet, we find her saying "Fortune forbid my outside have not charmed her". "Fortune" is a word Malvolio also uses to describe what he thinks are his prospects "'Tis but fortune; all is fortune." Maria's letter has led him to believe "Thy Fates open their hands." His response is to thank "my stars ... Jove and my stars be praised." The Elizabethans firmly believed their futures were written in the stars. Are we to think of Malvolio as innocent in his belief that "Jove, not I, is the doer of this, and he is to be thanked" ... and recognise it as mitigation?

Olivia too, falling in love with Cesario, comes out with what is clearly a belief in Providence:

> Fate, show thy force; ourselves we do not owe.
> What is decreed must be, and be this so.
>
> (Act I, scene 5, 300-1)

It is not without a certain irony, when we consider the letter's advice to Malvolio, that at the end of the play Olivia exhorts Cesario to "take thy fortunes up". Sebastian, landing on the seacoast, talks to his companion Antonio of fate, though somewhat glumly:

> My stars shine darkly
> over me. The malignancy of my fate might perhaps
> distemper yours; therefore I shall crave of you your
> leave, that I may bear my evils alone.
>
> (Act II, scene 1, 3-6)

(Sebastian, like Olivia and like Garbo, wants to be alone). He and Antonio become victims of time: Antonio has been a constant companion to Sebastian for three months – the time of the action of the play, a fact confirmed for us by the Duke's pointing to Cesario and saying "Three months this youth hath tended upon me." Antonio complains:

> ... for three months before
> No interim, not a minute's vacancy,
> Both day and night, did we keep company.
>
> (Act V, scene 1, 92-4)

and claims to have seen him (taking Viola for her brother) "Not half an hour before."

One could rightly claim that Viola is Providence's agent, in that without her arrival in Illyria or her decision to enter the action there would be no outcome or a very different one. However, one only has to consider the timing of the various characters' entrances in the final scene, for example, to realise that the part of Time is really being played by Shakespeare: it is he who presides over the action, arranging events, determining coincidences, playfully engineering mistaken identities, complicating things, putting on a sort of puppet show, pulling the strings and determining the way his characters behave in time and the way time may be said to use them. And he arranges his material into equations – parallels, correspondences, contrasts – out of which significances emerge. Or, to return to the metaphor with which we started this chapter, putting his characters comically into a state of dance and gently mocking their pretensions and ineptitudes. Over all, the aim, in Fabian's words, is ostensibly more to "pluck on laughter than revenge".

7

Wit, and't Be Thy Will

HAMLET How came he mad?
CLOWN Very strangely, they say.
HAMLET How strangely?
CLOWN Faith, e'en with losing his wits.
                (*Hamlet*, Act V, scene 1, 158-61)

To state something I hope is fairly obvious: one of the great pleasures in seeing and listening to, reading and re-reading Shakespeare, derives from the fact his language is so flexible that it becomes endlessly rich in meanings. This is largely because the culture he inhabits and expresses was in the habit of thinking analogically. Meanings, like ripples from a stone thrown into a pond, keep spreading outwards. The pleasure comes from seeing the ways in which so many things are linked or set up as opposites. The idea of white is contained within the word 'black'. It is these that provide the plays with their dynamic and the feeling of being something organic. We have already become aware of certain interlinkings: for example, melancholy, madness, drinking, drowning, weeping, 'corruption' of language (talking distractedly), the devil. We have also touched on opposites in the form of appearance/reality, folly/wisdom, modesty/pride, order/disorder, virtue/dishonour. In our epigraph from *Hamlet* we see 'wits' and madness balanced as opposites: understanding them and other opposites – as well as correspondences (including punning and parody) – is, as I hope we are making clear, important in *Twelfth Night*.

    In a culture that sets up reason as an ideal (the quality ascribed to the angelic orders is pure reason) it is not strange to find an anxiety over madness. The most potent exploration of this is *King Lear*; the most intriguing is *Hamlet*, packed with ambivalences, where the line between sanity and madness is difficult to draw.

Wit and Reason go hand in hand, and in a special sense there was a primary given to Reason in medieval thought. Reason was held to disclose the order of the universe. As A.N. Whitehead put it, the medieval world was an "age of faith based on reason". The philosopher Anselm thought the existence of God was provable from concepts alone, whilst our age – the 'scientific' age – is one of "reason based on faith". That is faith in scientific principles. Reason, and its cognate reasonableness, is also about balance and control. Mental health relies on the exercise of reason, just as reason is necessary to discern the order of the world. This is the conceptual fabric of Shakespeare's intellectual world. Faith was reasonable, and the Puritans, whether in their ecstatic 'enthusiastic' state (enthusiasm means filled with God) or sombre, were ridiculous, unbalanced people. Reason and Wit, are not only understanding order, but also restoring it.

In *Twelfth Night* there are a great many references to 'wit', 'wits', 'five wits'. They appear rather elastic in the way they are used. Feste, disguised as Sir Topas, asks Malvolio "Alas, sir, how fell you besides your five wits?" In other words, what caused you to go mad – madness being a tainting or a losing of one's wits. (For us moderns the word 'wit' more often than not simply means a kind of clever humour or denotes the person using it – though we still use 'wits' to suggest the power of reasoning). The expression 'five wits' has fallen out of use: *The Shorter Oxford English Dictionary* gives us "the five (bodily) senses; often vaguely the perceptions or mental faculties generally". In the play, 'five wits' seems to accord with the second half of this definition and can be taken to mean sanity/commonsense; it signifies the power to govern all one's faculties, to keep them in healthy check. Whatever the case, failure to do so is clearly harmful: it can lead to excess and madness.

Generally, 'wit' means intelligence and the God-given ability to use it. Feste and Viola are the best in the play at using their wit(s). Viola's serious punning, when she conflates Illyria and Elysium, tells us that intelligence has entered the play. Her intelligent assessment of the Captain is a just one "I believe thou hast a mind that suits/with this thy fair and outward character." In other words she recognises virtue and rewards it. Her decision to disguise herself for her own protection and seek employment with the Duke is entirely rational, even if an outcome cannot be foretold:

> What else may hap to time I will commit.
> Only shape thou thy silence to my wit.
>
> (Act I, scene 2, 61-2)

Here 'wit' suggests intention or plan. Her ability to recognise worth in others is in evidence after encountering Feste at the beginning of Act III and the gentle (and virtually equal) contest of wits they engage in there. Responding to Feste's:

> A sentence is
> but a cheveril glove to a good wit; how quickly the
> wrong side may be turned outward!
>
> (Act III, scene 1, 11-13)

she understands perfectly that "They that dally nicely with words may quickly make them wanton" and concludes, on Feste's exit, that:

> This fellow is wise enough to play the fool;
> And to do that well craves a kind of wit.
> He must observe their mood on whom he jests,
> The quality of persons, and the time,
> And, like the haggard, check at every feather
> That comes before his eye. This is a practice
> As full of labour as a wise man's art.
> For folly that he wisely shows is fit;
> But wise men, folly-fallen, quite taint their wit.
>
> (Act III, scene 1, 58-66)

Viola has her wits about her.

The first 'wit' denotes intelligence, the second commonsense. This speech is central to our understanding of the play. Recognising the difficulties inherent in the business of truth-telling (being misunderstood – deliberately or otherwise – or dismissively laughed at ... see Sebastian's reactions to Feste at the start of Act IV) and the skills required to fulfil the jester's function and escape whipping, offers a yardstick by which we judge the behaviour of the various characters. It is no small irony that the wise Feste is professionally and ambivalently a 'fool'. Wit and wisdom in him go hand in hand. As he tells Maria in Act I, scene 5, "God give them wisdom that have it; and those that are fools, let them use their talents." When Olivia comes on the scene he invokes wit as if it were a titular deity:

> Wit, an't be thy will, put me into good fooling.
> Those wits that think they have thee do very oft prove
> fools; and I that am sure I lack thee may pass for a wise
> man. For what says Quinapalus? 'Better a witty fool
> than a foolish wit.'
>
> (Act I, scene 5, 29-33)

Then looking Olivia straight in the eye says "God bless thee, lady!", clearly implying that *she's* the "foolish wit" of Quinapalus' saying! Again we have the see-saw equation between wisdom and folly and, in the largely affectionate ("my mouse of virtue") battle of wits that ensues, Olivia comes off second best, wittily proven to be the fool by virtue of her unhealthy mourning for her brother.

Toby and Andrew are abusers of wit as well as time. Aguecheek, naively caught in a perplexing game of puns around the word "accost", is intuitively aware of his own dull-wittedness, thinking he's maybe just about average ("no more wit than a Christian or an ordinary man") but foolishly believing his wit is dulled by eating beef.

Malvolio means something else by 'wit'. He recognises its connection with madness but seems to use it to mean decency, civility, proper behaviour. Dragged out of his bed to deal with the drunken rioters (among whom we find Feste too enjoying some licence) he demands:

> My masters, are you mad? Or what are you?
> Have you no wit, manners, nor honesty, but to gabble
> like tinkers at this time of night? Do ye make an ale-
> house of my lady's house, that ye squeak out your
> coziers' catches without any mitigation or remorse of
> voice? Is there no respect of place, persons, nor time in
> you?
>
> (Act II, scene 3, 85-91)

The questions are treated as rhetorical, the answer being a resounding No. In any case, Toby only hears the word "time" and wilfully twists it: "We did keep time, sir, in our catches". When Maria, devising her plan to gull Malvolio, uses the word "wit" it contains suggestions of deviousness:

> For Monsieur Malvolio, let me alone
> with him. If I do not gull him into a nayword, and make
> him a common recreation, do not think I have wit
> enough to lie straight in my bed. I know I can do it.
>
> (Act II, scene 3, 129-32)

In comparison to the letter she devises, what a poor exercise of wit the other letter offering a challenge to a duel is! And Malvolio's letter is exhibited later as proof of sanity. In the Sir Topas scene Feste uses the word "wits" to mean Malvolio's sanity ("e'er I will allow of thy wits"), as does Malvolio, convinced he is "as well in my wits as an man in Illyria", and who not unjustly feels everyone is out to make him mad, "face me out of my wits". And when, in the final scene, asked to read out Malvolio's letter (which the Duke considers sane, saying "This savours not much of distraction") Feste first of all puts on a madman's voice and is ordered to read it properly. Olivia tells him "Prithee read i'thy right wits".

Yet another opposite to wit is witchcraft and, though, as we have already said, there are no on-stage supernatural beings influencing the play's events, we do hear Antonio, brought before Orsino, saying "A witchcraft drew me hither". We might wish to remember Iago's boast in *Othello* that he works "by wit, and not by witchcraft". Witches are agents of the devil.

8

Are All the People Mad?

Illyria is a place of madness and misrule. Hence Sebastian's question. The answer to it is the Cheshire Cat's in *Alice in Wonderland*: "we're all mad here. I'm mad. You're mad." The exception, before the shipwrecked arrivals, being Feste, who, in a mad world, has enough skill and cunning to adjust to situations. In order to survive in a mad and dangerous world Viola has to make necessary adjustments; Sebastian simply experiences amazement.

Other people's sufferings – not to mention those of animals – have always provided us with spectacle (today reality television makes voyeurs of us vicariously enjoying others' discomforts and consequent bad behaviour). Mad persons are no exception: Bedlam Hospital where the insane were sent was visited by many for the simple purpose of marvelling and laughing at them. It is akin to applauding the suffering of animals, as in the bear- and bull-baiting theatres virtually in the same street as the Globe. The ruse to expose Malvolio is viewed as a sort of bear-baiting. In Act II, scene 5, Toby says "To anger him, we'll have the bear again, and we will fool him black and blue."

Illyria then is a kind of Bedlam. One form of treatment for madness was to confine the sufferer in a dark room. And this happens to Malvolio. He is further baited there, made a spectacle of, a laughing stock; the madman-parody of reading out his letter, until Olivia stops it, is meant as a continuation of the entertainment. Malvolio too is deceived into exposing a divided self … or is it his real self, a case of the "inbred malady in all of us", the original sin consequent on the Fall?

It is surely this "inbred malady" that the devil exploits. Madness is seen as a form of possession, being taken over, possessed, rapt, by evil spirits. Malvolio is meant to be shriven by Sir Topas, the priest:

> MALVOLIO   …
> Good Sir Topas, do not think I am mad. They have laid
> me here in hideous darkness –
> FESTE Fie, thou dishonest Satan! I call thee by the most
> modest terms, for I am one of those gentle ones that will
> use the devil himself with courtesy. Sayst thou that
> house is dark?
> MALVOLIO As hell, Sir Topas.
>
>   (Act IV, scene 2, 29-35)

This equating of madness with Satan is comically treated and we laugh on a there-but-for-the-grace-of-God-go-I basis. But it is no joke: the language is not figurative but real. What we read as metaphor Elizabethan audiences considered, to use words from earlier, interlinked correspondences. Let's consider the following passage in which what I'm calling correspondences is grossly and deliberately misunderstood:

> SIR TOBY   I did think by
> the excellent constitution of thy leg it was formed under
> the star of a galliard.
> SIR ANDREW Ay, 'tis strong, and it does indifferent well
> in a dun-coloured stock. Shall we set about some revels?
> SIR TOBY What shall we do else? Were we not born under
> Taurus?
> SIR ANDREW Taurus? That's sides and heart.
> SIR TOBY No, sir, it is legs and thighs. Let me see thee
> caper.
>
>   (Act I, scene 3, 124-33)

The talk here is of the connection, in the audience's mind, between the parts of the body and the constellations (the stars of the zodiac) on which theories of behaviour relied. As Tillyard tells us in *The Elizabethan World Picture*:

> Characteristically both speakers are made to get the association
> wrong; and Shakespeare probably knew that to Taurus were
> assigned the neck and throat. There is irony in Sir Toby's being

34

right in a way he did not mean. He meant to refer to dancing – legs and thighs – but the drinking implied by neck and throat is just as apt to the proposed revels ... the serious and ceremonious game of the Middle Ages has degenerated into farce.

Ignorance (equated with darkness in Feste's remark "there is no darkness but ignorance") is another of the faces of madness or at least is productive of it, as we shall see when we consider disguise and various forms of mistakenness – in other words, ignorance as untruth, which is only put right when time untangles the knot and reason prevails.

Most of the characters live in ignorance of, or artfully disguise, their true selves. It is this ambivalence which is at the heart of drama. In comedy, to see people acting out of character or having their 'real' characters exposed is humorous. In tragedy it is painful. Gain in one, loss in the other.

"Madness in great ones must not unwatchèd go" says Claudius in *Hamlet*. And part of the fun of *Twelfth Night* is witnessing the nobly-born behaving badly and madly, out of character or, hypocritically, getting entangled in complications of their own making.

The play contains a Duke, a Countess, two Knights and the genteel Viola and Sebastian (Viola/Cesario tells Olivia her parentage is "Above my fortunes, yet my state is well./I am a gentleman.")

In Olivia we have a Countess who looks as though she's been made anxious about men; her brother and father leave her defenceless; she is unable to put any trust in her dissolute uncle and has handed most of the responsibility for handling her affairs over to her steward and her handmaid. She is also under siege: the Duke is pestering her and her uncle has brought an idiot knight, a potential wooer, into the house.

On the whole the 'lesser' characters are the more resilient: Maria has her head screwed on, Malvolio is no fool until gulled into being one, the Captain and Antonio are good-hearted rescuers, Cesario a dutiful go-between, Feste adapts himself to circumstances – as Viola says of him:

He must observe their mood on whom he jests,
The quality of persons, and the time,

And, like the haggard, check at every feather
That comes before his eye.

(Act III, scene 1, 60-3)

Maria has no illusions about Sir Andrew Aguecheek. Nor do we, confronted with such a name. One definition of 'ague' in the *Shorter Oxford Dictionary* is "malarial fever, with paroxysms, consisting of a hot, a cold, and a sweating stage." Shivering and twitching then – at one with the motif of illness that runs through the play – in someone from whom one might perhaps catch infection, as well as perhaps implying (he has yellow hair) cowardice. Sir Toby is callously fleecing him of money, in the supposed role of go-between (think of the contrast in Cesario's outraged response to Olivia, "I am no fee'd post, lady; keep your purse.") Toby is more bawd than go-between and in addition, with Aguecheek as accomplice, he has good excuses for his drunkenness: "Th'art a scholar! Let us therefore eat and drink." According to him, Aguecheek (though privately to Maria he insultingly calls him "Agueface") has "all the good gifts of nature", to which Maria replies "He hath indeed all, most natural." Such is the complexity of Elizabethan language that one of the meanings of 'natural' is idiot. Sir Andrew, a man generally innocent of meanings, ironically uses this word of himself. Comparing his wit with that of Sir Toby he tells Feste (who really does know all about it) that in fooling, Toby "does it with a better grace, but I do it more natural" – in other words more like a natural-born idiot. Maria knows that, though Andrew hasn't much to show by way of brains, he is as intemperate as Sir Toby:

> he's a fool, he's a great quarreller; and but that he hath
> the gift of a coward to allay the gust he hath in quarrel-
> ling, 'tis thought among the prudent he would quickly
> have the gift of a grave.

(Act I, scene 3, 27-30)

Once Sir Andrew, with his striking straight yellow hair, makes his entrance, it is apparent that she is correct in her judgement. The audience has been primed to expect an idiot and is not disappointed. He barely understands what is being said to him. In this scene Maria teases him, taking on the role of Clown, and her target is an easy one to hit. Toby's sexual innuendoes are lost on him, as are her verbal jabs. He is made to confess his dull-wittedness – though he blames it on eating too much beef – and admit that he has wasted time in "masques and revels ... fencing, dancing, and bear-baiting." He is one character in the play unlikely to benefit by changing for the better. He will always be a gull and a dolt. Such is his feeble-mindedness that, when he threatens to pack his bags and take himself off home, Toby has no difficulty in dissuading him with talk of galliards and cutting a caper.

Sir Toby's first words in the play (characters' first words are usually telling) constitute a curse ("What a plague means my niece ... ?"); Malvolio's are sternly censorious: the gentle baiting of Olivia by the Clown is heavily rounded on. When she asks "What do you think of this fool, Malvolio? Doth he not mend?" his reply is:

> Yes, and shall do, till the pangs of death shake
> him. Infirmity, that decays the wise, doth ever make the
> better fool.
>
> (Act I, scene 5, 70-2)

9

I'll Serve This Duke

Viola says she will offer herself to the Duke's service as a musician. Her first thought had been service with Olivia. Thankfully this is forestalled by the Captain's:

> That were hard to compass,
> Because she will admit no kind of suit,
> No, not the Duke's.
>
> (Act I, scene 2, 45-7)

This information tells her that, in paying suit to the Countess, the Duke is safely in love and therefore not a sexual threat to her. However, it does mean that if she is to protect her maidenly honour (her virginity as well as her status) and make her way:

> Till I had made mine own occasion mellow –
> What my estate is.
>
> (Act I, scene 2, 44-5)

she needs, in a world ostensibly governed by men, to conceal her feminine nature. The irony of course is she that falls for the Duke. Let's remind ourselves that on-stage we have a boy actor playing the role of a woman disguised as a boy falling in love with a man. Amusing to us as this clearly is, it was obviously more so to its original audience.

Why does Viola fall for him? We have met him already and found him behaving like a melancholy madman.

Aside from the fact that people tend to fall in love spontaneously, there are certain factors to consider: she knows before encountering him that he is a bachelor, that he is already romantically primed, and

that Olivia, to whom he is paying court, is yet a "virtuous maid".
In a matter of three days, an extraordinary intimacy develops between
Cesario and his/her master. Valentine comments on it:

> If the Duke continue these favours towards
> you, Cesario, you are like to be much advanced. He hath
> known you but three days, and already you are no
> stranger.
>
> (Act I, scene 4, 1-4)

The Duke himself, obviously finding something very attractively
trustworthy in her, admits:

> I have unclasped
> To thee the book even of my secret soul.
>
> (Act I, scene 4, 13-14)

Secrecy is part of the code of courtly lovers and for Orsino to
reveal his "secret soul" to Cesario after a matter of only three days is
extraordinary. (We are right to suspect he's already, though far from
aware of it, on the road to finding his true love). She thinks it
important to ask "Is he inconstant, sir, in his favours?" and is
comforted by Valentine's reply "No, believe me." Does this really
square, though, with Orsino's totally irresponsible command (he is
after all the man supposed to be governing Illyria, the enforcer of its
laws) that she break the law in her mission to Olivia's house?

> Be clamorous and leap all civil bounds
> Rather than make unprofited return.
>
> (Act I, scene 4, 21-2)

There is obvious irony in his parting words:

> Prosper well in this,
> And thou shalt live as freely as thy lord,
> To call his fortunes thine.
>
> (Act I, scene 4, 38-40)

It almost sounds like a proposal of marriage.
Viola has, in a matter of three days, fallen in love with him, either

by letting love (which we know is blind) come in through the eyes or by falling for something in the Duke that we haven't seen in action but may at some level have inferred. In other words if, as we have already suggested, he is victim of a divided self, she sees the true side of his character, a potential self (what ironically people refer to as 'old self'), the one to be regained in the recovering of his wits. This is a matter for a director and actor to decide.

Yet in many ways Orsino is not a likeable character: he is moody, imperious and dangerous when crossed. In Act V he finally shifts himself to visit Olivia; and in doing so may be said to be entering the real world. But before his encounter with the object of his love or love-object he has to cross the bridge, as it were, of Feste and engage in a banter of wits, during which he is gently cajoled into doubling – but not trebling – the tip he gives. And not before the arrested Antonio is brought before him, for whose manly honour he generously shows respect:

> That face of his I do remember well
> Yet when I saw it last, it was besmeared
> As black as Vulcan in the smoke of war.
> A baubling vessel was he captain of,
> For shallow draught and bulk, unprizable;
> With which, such scatheful grapple did he make
> With the most noble bottom of our fleet,
> That very envy and the tongue of loss
> Cried fame and honour on him.
>
> (Act V, scene 1, 48-56)

However when Olivia appears Orsino reverts to being the besotted man the play started with. His language once more is hyperbolic: "Here comes the Countess; now heaven walks on earth." As far as we can tell it is the first time he has cast eyes on her for at least three months . Olivia rejects him, asserting her "constancy" in response to his accusation "Still so cruel?" She is of course strengthened in her attitude by the fact that she is, as it were, otherwise engaged. His outburst of temper – now that he has refusal directly from her lips – is extremely violent. One could say he has been given a wake-up call:

What, to perverseness? You uncivil lady,
To whose ingrate and unauspicious altars
My soul the faithfull'st offerings have breathed out
That e'er devotion tendered!

> (Act V, scene 1, 110-13)

'Civil' and 'uncivil' are important words in this play. The obvious question to ask of the above is: if Orsino thinks this of Olivia why does he love her? Well, of course, he doesn't; he merely thinks the courtly love code is de rigeur. In any case, if as we have implied he is on a learning curve, then he is about to discover that the cruelty he sees as a necessary part of the ennobling suffering of courtly lovers (who constantly complain of it) and the real 'cruelty' of the real woman, Olivia, are far from being the same. But not before he comes out with the extraordinary statement (which pre-echoes Othello) that he could contemplate killing the one he purports to love:

Why should I not – had I the heart to do it –
Like to th'Egyptian thief at point of death
Kill what I love – a savage jealousy
That sometime savours nobly?

> (Act V, scene 1, 115-18)

(The reference to the "Egyptian thief" is from a story in Heliodorus' *Ethopica,* a Greek romance translated in 1569, in which a bandit, Thyamis, besieged in a cave, threatens to kill a captive princess who rejects his love). We must remember the presence of others in this scene, above all the quiet ("my duty hushes me") Viola. What can she be thinking of Orsino's behaviour here – or aren't we supposed to ask? His mood is wildly vindictive (it is worth keeping Malvolio in mind, as someone who has more – more real – reason to claim vengeance):

Since you to non-regardance cast my faith,
And that I partly know the instrument
That screws me from my true place in your favour,
Live you the marble-breasted tyrant still.

> (Act V, scene 1, 119-122)

41

and pointing to Cesario/Viola continues with:

> But this your minion, whom I know you love,
> And whom, by heaven, I swear, I tender dearly,
> Him will I tear out of that cruel eye
> Where he sits crownèd in his master's spite.
> Come, boy, with me, my thoughts are ripe in mischief.
> I'll sacrifice the lamb that I do love
> To spite a raven's heart within a dove.
>
> (Act V, scene 1, 123-9)

There is an obvious change in his language – though hate as much as love has its own rhetoric. We have to ask who is now really being cruel? Viola's retort contains, if we are to assume the sexual meaning Elizabethans attached to the word 'die', a defiantly sexual taunt, possibly looking forward to her marriage bed:

> And I, most jocund, apt, and willingly
> To do you rest, a thousand deaths would die.
>
> (Act V, scene 1, 130-1)

Cesario/Viola, about to follow Orsino out, is checked by Olivia's "Where goes Cesario?", to which the reply is about as public a statement of her love for Orsino that the play can yet allow outside soliloquy:

> After him I love
> More than I love these eyes, more than my life,
> More by all mores than e'er I shall love wife.
> If I do feign, you witnesses above,
> Punish my life, for tainting of my love!
>
> (Act V, scene 1, 132-6)

Note the word "feign". Viola is one of those who follow Edgar's advice at the end of *King Lear* to "Speak what we feel, not what we ought to say."

The question remains how can she fall for such a character as Orsino?

When she first makes her declaration in Act I, Shakespeare merely allows her a rhyming-couplet aside: "Yet a barful strife!/Whoe'er I woo, myself would be his wife". This could simply be taken as

Shakespeare, in his building up of complications, determining that the plot at this exact point requires no more than such a statement; and expecting the audience to work out motives for themselves. But in view of the Duke's behaviour and pronouncements she is witness to during the course of the play, the question, as we have said, remains.

It is precisely the fact Viola speaks two languages (parody of her master's courtly love clichés alternating with her own authentic voice) that enables the attraction felt by Olivia to develop. If the play contains characters who are victims of what I'm calling the divided self, who tend to express themselves in 'wrong' or feigned language, there are also those who, in their need to make their way in the world, must handle two kinds of language, who are able to shift skilfully and without compromise from one to the other. Feste is one, Viola another. Viola/Cesario tells Olivia she has "taken great pains" to study Orsino's message and that it is "poetical". Olivia's response is "It is more likely to be feigned." This shows that she has a capability of separating the false from the true. She falls, not for the false poetry of Orsino's "adorations ... fertile tears ... groans that thunder love ... sighs of fire", but the fresher lyricism of:

> Make me a willow cabin at your gate,
> And call upon my soul within the house;
> Write loyal cantons of contemnèd love
> And sing them loud even in the dead of night;
>
> (Act I, scene 5, 257-60)

It also demonstrates how quickly her vow to "abjure the sight and company of men" goes out of the window! It doesn't take long before she is tempted into the dishonour, the untruth of sending the ring ... ironically a symbol of unity and eternity. Viola's reaction is to say "Disguise, I see thou art a wickedness/Wherein the pregnant enemy does much" ... the "pregnant enemy" being none other than the devil. Disguise is another form of possession, of madness, but at least we can say she is aware of the fact and of its dangers. But locked in disguise she is; and it creates real suffering for her (as opposed to Orsino's 'feigned' and fashion-driven suffering), having to listen to the gross self-pitying implied in the song "Come away, come away, death", and to his imperious protestations.

Unrequited love is both a torture and a challenge. To Orsino, Olivia is unavailable, happily unattainable: he is content to languish at home and suffer his sovereign cruelty's proud rejection of him – it's part of the game; to Olivia, Cesario is unavailable (for reasons more obvious to the audience) and it is not long before she experiences rejection and starts flinging accusations of pride at him/her. It is not without irony that Olivia at one minute rejects Cesario ("Be not afraid, good youth, I will not have you") and in another says:

> Yet come again; for thou perhaps mayst move
> That heart, which now abhors, to like his love.
> (Act III, scene 1, 160-1)

This is yet a further example of how the infection of love makes lovers inconstant, changeable in their affections – seeing not with the mind but with the eyes:

> My master loves her dearly;
> And I, poor monster, fond as much on him;
> And she, mistaken, seems to dote on me.
> What will become of this? As I am man,
> My state is desperate for my master's love.
> As I am woman – now, alas the day,
> What thriftless sighs shall poor Olivia breathe!
> (Act II, scene 2, 33-9)

But she is at least aware of her situation and while she keeps the faith in providence that is characteristic of her there is hope.

10

Conceal Me What I Am

It is said that what Shakespeare consistently explores in his plays is the relationship of appearance to reality, the disparity between what seems and what is. It is the very stuff of theatre. The dramatist provides a text in order to create an illusion played out on a stage; actors put on make-up and costume and become something they are not; words create imaginary locations and scenery[1]; in-jokes are possible like Fabian's "If this were played upon a stage now, I could condemn it as an improbable fiction" or Olivia's "Are you a comedian?"; plays within plays can occur (Malvolio's appearance in cross-gartered stockings is an equivalent); the ambiguities of words are exploited; audience expectations aroused and either teasingly frustrated or happily satisfied. We have already noted how boy actors playing women's parts add further levels of illusion.

Orsino and Olivia live in illusory worlds: the world of courtly love and the world of protracted "sad remembrance". They are unhealthy places, given over to delusion. Viola, to survive, to maintain her sanity and protect her honour, enters these illusory worlds as an illusion ("Conceal me what I am"). Like Feste she travels between them, confirming their illusions while at the same time (one might say she invades them) undermining and subverting them.

Toby and Andrew live in a pretend Peter Pan world, one in which they refuse to grow up and where there is – as in the imaginary country of Cockaigne (which *The Shorter Oxford Dictionary* describes as an "abode of luxury and idleness") – a plentiful supply of cakes and ale. Toby's vision of Sir Andrew is wilfully unreal, as we have seen when contrasting it with Maria's. The world Toby and Andrew create and inhabit clashes discordantly with Olivia's would-be cloistress-world. In fact, all the various worlds in this play end up colliding. They are also put to the test by the agents of wit. Olivia's reasons for mourning her brother's death, for example, are easily demolished by Feste, and his criticism of the Duke, implied in his comment that he'd have "men of such constancy put to sea, that their business might be everything, and their intent everywhere; for that's it that always makes a good voyage of nothing", hits the nail bang on the head.

Antonio has to make his way cautiously in what to him is literally a hostile world; Sebastian barges into the middle of it (after three months of sight-seeing!) disbelievingly:

> What relish is in this? How runs the stream?
> Or I am mad, or else this is a dream.
> Let fancy still my sense in Lethe steep;
> If it be thus to dream, still let me sleep!
>
> (Act IV, scene 1, 59-62)

Malvolio is gulled into behaving ludicrously out of character and walks himself into a nightmare.

When Cesario is first allowed into the Countess's presence, Olivia disguises herself with a veil. It doesn't take long however before it's discarded. In this scene there is much interplay of the appearance/reality theme. In answer to Olivia's "Are you a comedian?" (actor) we hear:

> VIOLA   No, my profound heart; and yet by the very fangs
>   of malice, I swear I am not that I play. Are you the lady
>   of the house?
> OLIVIA   If I do not usurp myself, I am.
>
> (Act I, scene 5, 176-9)

Asked "What are you? What would you?" Cesario replies, "What I am and what I would are as secret as maidenhead." Then comes discussion of the contrast between plain speaking and 'feigned' 'poetical' utterance. And all of it is a game of wits, a bantering play with truths, which however, begins to turn nasty with Olivia's unveiling and her question "Is't not well done?" to which Cesario returns "Excellently done – if God did all!" And soon enough Viola comes to the conclusion "I see you what you are, you are too proud." In Act III, when Olivia asks "I prithee, tell me what thou think'st of

me?" the answer is "That you do think you are not what you are" –
in other words, you are deluded in thinking you're in love with a
man. The interchange continues:

> OLIVIA If I think so, I think the same of you.
> VIOLA   Then you think right; I am not what I am.
> OLIVIA I would you were as I would have you be.
> VIOLA   Would it be better, madam, than I am?
>   I wish it might, for now I am your fool.
>
> (Act III, scene 1, 137-41)

Needless to say, Olivia cannot for a whole complex of reasons
see Viola/Cesario for what she/he is. It is only in soliloquy or asides
that Viola can be what she is. Olivia's condition is a complicated
mess: she loves a cross-dressed woman, is besieged by Orsino, and
her house, in which there is another would-be wooer, is in a condition
of misrule. How, indeed, will this fadge? She has caught the infection
of love; what was to be reserved for her brother has now been
deflected elsewhere. She is about to do something quite dishonourable
by lyingly sending Malvolio after Cesario with a ring. His/her
summing up of Olivia's plight is:

> I left no ring with her; what means this lady?
> Fortune forbid my outside have not charmed her!
> She made good view of me, indeed so much
> That – methought – her eyes had lost her tongue,
> For she did speak in starts, distractedly.
>
> (Act II, scene 2, 17-21)

Note the effect on language ("in starts, distractedly") and Viola's
sincere hope "my outside have not charmed her" – physical attraction
(far from the ideal of a 'marriage of true minds') and 'charm' denoting
a state of enchantment (linking up with the ideas of madness and
possession and Antonio's word "witchcraft"). But Viola is in just as
bad a fix. Remember her lines:

> … My master loves her dearly;
> And I, poor monster, fond as much on him;
> And she, mistaken, seems to dote on me.
> What will become of this? As I am man,

My state is desperate for my master's love.
As I am woman – now, alas the day,
What thriftless sighs shall poor Olivia breathe!

(Act II, scene 2, 33-9)

Note here the phrase "poor monster" denoting her equivocal condition of being both male and female but also indicating betrayal to a behaviour deemed less than human.

You could perhaps say that Malvolio's yellow cross-gartered stockings is a kind of disguise, in that he appears other than his manifest self in them. Certainly Feste is himself and other than himself in his fooling and in the disguise of Sir Topas. Putting on a gown and beard at Maria's behest he says:

Well, I'll put it on and I will dissemble myself in't,
and I would I were the first that ever dissembled in such
a gown.

(Act IV, scene 2, 4-6)

And, once disguised, he says "that that is, is. So I, being Master Parson, am Master Parson; for what is 'that' but 'that'? And 'is' but 'is'?" a further example of the appearance/reality theme that helps, with other threads, to thread the play together.

Note
[1] See the Prologue to Shakespeare's *Henry V*.

11

Suppose Him Virtuous

High on any list of Elizabethan ideals will be found the pursuit of virtue and honour, especially among the gentler (as in gentleman) sort. So at this point let's consider where goodness is located in the play. As so often with other aspects, we will discover it largely through contrast.

Olivia supposes Orsino virtuous, knows him to be noble,

> Of great estate, of fresh and stainless youth,
> In voices well divulged, free, learned, and valiant,
> And in dimension and the shape of nature
> A gracious person.
>
> (Act I, scene 5, 248-51)

She portrays him – in a way similar to Ophelia of Prince Hamlet – as the ideal Renaissance prince ... but the word "suppose" shows that her knowledge of him has almost certainly come to her second-hand, by report, or is something simply assumed. It could well be they have never met or have only seen each other at a distance. Contrast this with Viola's estimation of the Captain:

> There is a fair behaviour in thee, Captain,
> And though that nature with a beauteous wall
> Doth oft close in pollution, yet of thee
> I will believe thou hast a mind that suits
> With this thy fair and outward character.
>
> (Act I, scene 2, 48-52)

In other words, she is not taken in by outward appearances – though the Captain is actually fortunate in being simultaneously both good-looking and virtuous; her judgement of character is rooted in direct experience. She recognises goodness and immediately wishes to reward it.

Feste calls Olivia his "mouse of virtue" – which is surprisingly affectionate, if gently critical – accusing her of coyly hiding her beauty from the world. Virtue and beauty are connected and this connection, between outward and moral beauty, is again in question when Olivia unveils: on seeing her face, Cesario comments "Excellently done, if God did all." This reminds one of Hamlet's unkind – though not uncommon for the time – remarks to Ophelia:

> I have heard of your paintings, well enough. God hath
> given you one face, and you make yourselves another.
>
> (*Hamlet*, Act II, scene 1, 144-5)

We have posited the idea of divided selves expressed in different registers of language as a way of judging the play's characters. (Antonio's question "How have you made division of yourself?" would make a good epigraph for the play). Olivia reveals something of her true nature when she chides Malvolio for his intemperate and over-solemn judgement of Feste. In an un-mouselike way she roundly puts him in his place:

> O, you are sick of self-love, Malvolio, and taste
> with a distempered appetite. To be generous, guiltless,
> and of free disposition, is to take those things for bird-
> bolts that you deem cannon bullets.
>
> (Act I, scene 5, 85-8)

Though she may not be able to see the faults in her own behaviour, she does seem to evince here a generosity of spirit and an ability to see faults in others. There is also kind-heartedness and compassion in her reaction to the sight of Malvolio in his yellow stockings:

> Good Maria, let this fellow be looked to ...
> Let some of my people have a special care
> of him. I would not have him miscarry for the half of
> my dowry.
>
> (Act III, scene 4, 61-4)

... although it is quite possible for an actor to play these lines, as

John Lucas has suggested to me, with a supercilious giggle.

And with the first appearance of Cesario, we discover she is open to curiosity. Malvolio, no judge of character, is a cynic (can Feste ever be said to be cynical?) who can only speak slightingly of others. He describes Cesario as being

> Not yet old enough for a man, nor young
> enough for a boy; as a squash is before 'tis a peascod, or
> a codling when 'tis almost an apple. 'Tis with him in
> standing water between boy and man. He is very well-
> favoured, and he speaks very shrewishly. One would
> think his mother's milk were scarce out of him.
>
> (Act I, scene 5, 151-6)

In fact his derogatory remarks ironically serve to fire the Countess's curiosity, enabling her simply to indulge perhaps in further entertainment "for want of other idleness".

Loyalty and friendship are clear indications of the good: for example, the relationship between Sebastian and Antonio is something the play tests and affirms. The words "love" and "adore" are, without implying anything sexual, unashamedly used. The scene in which we meet them (Act II, scene 1) and the later entrusting of the purse, indicate a friendship based on gratitude, good faith (a "conscience firm") and an anxiety for the other's welfare. It affords something of a parallel to the scene between Viola and the Captain. The contrast is with Toby and Aguecheek, in whose relationship there is little by way of virtue. In fact Sir Toby uses the word "virtuous" in the sense of something opposed to his view of what life is all about. Sneering at Malvolio, he famously states "'Dost thou think, because thou art virtuous, there shall be no more cakes and ale?" Honour, in terms of manliness, is tried and tested in the matter of the duel. In Toby's opinion "there is no love-broker in the world can more prevail in man's commendation with woman than report of valour", as the appearance of Sebastian in Act II, scene 1, may be said to testify.

Olivia and Orsino have been, or have allowed themselves to be, seduced by 'wrong' attitudes to virtue and honour, which put them in a state of melancholia. Their devotion to excess in the end proves superficial – though their 'disguised' *real* selves are naturally rooted in them. Each rapidly strikes up – or, in the case of Olivia, attempts to – a telling intimacy with Viola/Cesario involving trust. Viola to the Duke's question "What dost thou know?" is able to make the confident rejoinder:

> Too well what love women to men may owe.
> In faith, they are as true of heart as we.
>
> (Act II, scene 4, 104-5)

Cesario in his/her interviews with Olivia, finds it frustratingly impossible to assert her virtue, what we perhaps might call integrity, expressing it thus:

> By innocence I swear, and by my youth,
> I have one heart, one bosom, and one truth.
> And that no woman has, nor never none
> Shall mistress be of it, save I alone.
>
> (Act III, scene 1, 154-7)

In Act III she is equally assertive about her integrity in reply to Antonio's Christ-like "Will you deny me now?" Her spirited answer is:

> I hate ingratitude more in a man
> Than lying, vainness, babbling drunkenness,
> Or any taint of vice whose strong corruption
> Inhabits our frail blood –
>
> (Act III, scene 4, 345-8)

Honest confessions at the end, particularly Fabian's, help to bring the play to a virtuous close.

12

Sometimes He is a Kind of Puritan

Malvolio. It is a harsh name, a prediction of malevolence. One might think of its belonging to the villain, the malcontent, wickedly engineering downfalls in a Jacobean revenge tragedy. The only downfall Malvolio brings about is his own and that is something he survives. We expect worse than we perhaps get. He is not actively malevolent. Like dull care, he is an enemy to life but only when pushed. Heavy-handed he may be but, when we first meet him, he is much exercised by the antics of the agents of "uncivil rule" Olivia has in her household. He is a dutiful steward, on the side of order, and his serious-to-the-point-of-solemnity character is useful in suiting the sad-remembrance mood of his mistress, who tells us "He is sad and civil,/And suits well for a servant with my fortunes." Charles Lamb's famous view of Malvolio is that he

> is not essentially ludicrous. He becomes comic by accident.
> He is cold, austere, repelling; but dignified, consistent, and,
> for what appears, rather of an overstretched morality … We
> see no reason why he should not have been brave, honourable,
> accomplished.

Kenneth Muir maintains that this view has led what he calls "some armchair critics" astray. Dover Wilson suggests that "There is no evidence that Shakespeare himself felt any tenderness for Malvolio". The play, however, shows otherwise. What we therefore need to assess is what degree of sympathy for him is warranted.

For those people who expect their comedy to be uproariously funny he is the centre of the play. Few things are funnier than the bringing down of pomposity and pretension and the exposure of accompanying hypocrisies. The play prepares us for what is going to happen (Maria's forged letter), so our expectations are satisfyingly fulfilled. It's just a matter of waiting for it. Timing is all. Poetic justice is going to be dished out. However, poetic justice and real justice are not always the same. The scene in the garden with Malvolio in yellow cross-gartered stockings and sporting an out-of-character smile is unfailingly hilarious, a wonderful piece of theatre.

If we attach a special significance to first words, then we have to say that Malvolio's immediately set him up as "an enemy to life". He belittles Feste's wit by equating it with dotage, declaring that "Infirmity, that decays the wise, doth ever make the better fool". It shows clearly that he himself has no sense of humour; he goes as far as to maintain that those who laugh at clowns like Feste are "no better than the fools' zanies" (i.e. than clowns' assistants). This, spoken to Olivia, is a direct criticism of her and provokes a sharp rebuke. It is Malvolio's lack of humour which is his major failing, providing a target for those who see it as threatening their licence to misrule. As we have noted earlier, it is something for us to respect in Olivia that she smartly rebukes him for his over-solemnity, giving us the key, not only to his character but also to those of others in the play, in telling him "O, you are sick of self-love, Malvolio, and taste with a distempered appetite" … an accusation (note the references to illness and food) that we have already been able to level at the Duke and Olivia herself.

Earlier we noticed how Malvolio's description of Cesario/Viola, seeking to be admitted to her presence, actually makes Olivia, in spite of her vow, curious to see the Duke's messenger. When their eventual interview is over and the fatal attraction has been established, Malvolio is required to "Run after that same peevish messenger" with a ring. This adjective "peevish" applies more to him than Cesario. We hear him quite untruthfully saying "Come, sir, you peevishly threw it to her" and then high-handedly and insultingly throwing it on the ground. "If it be worth stooping for, there it lies in your eye; if not, be it his that finds it." Stooping implies an act of shame and dishonour and shows that Malvolio regards Cesario his inferior. We need to add haughtiness and snobbery and telling lies – though it may be that this is what, exposed to, he has learnt or felt obliged to acquire – to our list of his vices.

When ordered in to deal with the caterwauling of we-three, he is on the side of sense, decency, and order. But this is because he has aspirations to move up the social scale and here, standing in for Olivia, may be said to be rehearsing the role he aspires to. It is tempting to look for mitigations for Malvolio, as Lamb has done, especially when we consider the treatment meted out to him as something liberal taste tends to judge unfair.

By the same token, it is easy, too tempting to provide excuses for the behaviour of Toby and Aguecheek. Bakhtin's concept of 'Carnival' has been put to use to show, in the words of Ramon Selden, that

> Toby represents the pure spirit of Carnival bent on mocking the narrow and life-denying face of Lent as represented by the 'Puritan' Malvolio ... Toby's riotousness and Malvolio's disapproval are the typical embodiment of the conflict between Carnival and Lent ... Toby displays a flagrant disrespect for convention, middle-class 'virtue' and the moral restraint imposed from above. In this he shares the plebeian (the common people's) refusal to accept the 'civilized' social order imposed by ruling élites of all kinds, a refusal expressed in popular festivities and holidays when the collective life of the people bubbles up and temporarily turns the world upside down. A conventional view of Toby's commitment to a life of 'cakes and ale' might suggest that the common people's culture is escapist, self-indulgent and coarse. This Lenten attitude has afflicted many critics in the past. The emphasis upon Carnival is not so much an indulgent attitude as a view 'from below' of the ruling class's severe and repressive moral and social attitudes. Carnivalised literature preserves something of this almost invisible counter-culture.

This is all well and good but we must remember that Toby and Aguecheek are knights of the realm – like Falstaff, dissolute members of the ruling class and not of the common people. That is unless we think of them as having opted for a kind of tavern culture or accept the implications of the play's title and consider them representative figures from the allowed festivities of Twelfth Night, imagine them 'elected' to office for the duration (of the festivities and of the play), after which, with the permitted topsy-turvyness over, the prevailing social order is restored. In other words, a period of licence which is in actuality an exercise in state control – a sort of safety valve – after which life is meant to be serious again. More likely, these two reprobates are incorrigibly attached to a life that refuses to become grown up, in an almost utopian freedom we all imagine and secretly envy. Toby is fortunate in not having to experience the reality-check Falstaff receives from Hal as newly-crowned King Henry V:

> I know thee not, old man. Fall to thy prayers.
> How ill white hairs become a fool and jester!
> (*Henry IV, Part II*, Act V, scene 22, 51-2,)

We might perhaps predict something of a change in Toby when he tells Maria "I would we were well rid of this knavery" and in his recognition that "I am now so far in offence with my niece that I cannot pursue this sport to the upshot"; perhaps in his statement, after being beaten, "I hate a drunken rogue" and in that he is 'rewarded' with marriage to Maria. As for Sir Andrew Aguecheek, the play simply abandons him, doesn't give him a second thought; his fate's unknown; we don't imagine him waking tomorrow morn as a wiser and a better man. As John Wain notes, when the play ends in "joy and benevolence", they "do not gather in the entire roll-call of characters. Sir Andrew, and of course Malvolio, are outside the happy circle." A less sympathetic assessment of Toby's role can be found in Greenblatt, who desribes him as:

> a parasite who sponges off his niece, ruthlessly gulls his supposed friend Sir Andrew, and richly deserves the thrashing he receives at the hands of an effeminate boy he thought he could bully.

It is Maria who calls Malvolio a Puritan. However, she qualifies it with the phrase "a kind of". By 'Puritan' she means no more than someone, in Muir's words, who "disapproves of harmless pleasures" – strait-laced, fastidious, censorious. It has proved a misleading epithet: it carries few of the Victorian connotations contained in the word 'puritanical'. And, though it may be read as a presage of the English Revolution when the Puritans got their way and theatres were closed, it is not really a term to be taken seriously in a theological sense. As Maurice Ashley has written: "At the beginning of the 17th century there was no such thing as a Puritan 'party'. There were sects starting to form: Presbyterians, Baptists, Congregationalists. But probably none of these Puritan sects was numerically strong in the first years of the 17th century ... the Puritans were an active but disunited Protestant minority." Minority they may have been but they were a vocal one and, in their belief that fiction was a species of lying, were opposed to play-going, wishing to instead close down the theatres, as dens of vice. As Muir puts it, "Elizabethan actors and dramatists had no reason to love Puritans because of their opposition to the stage". The word was enough to encourage the audience's derision. In the words of John Hale:

> When Olivia's puritanical and order-loving steward Malvolio in *Twelfth Night* reprimanded Sir Toby Belch for his noisy drinking, Shakespeare provided the tipsy knight with a celebrated retort: 'Dost thou think, because thou art virtuous there shall be no more cakes and ale?' It was a reply to delight an audience aware that even by attending a play they were incurring Malvolian disapproval.

Malvolio is not *technically* a Puritan, simply enough like one to be the focus of derision. Interestingly, the play does contain a reference to one Robert Browne (Sir Andrew says "I had as lief be a Brownist as a politician") who, as Ashley tells us, "presided over a 'congregational' church at Norwich ... He ... believed that the State should enforce and uphold their own favoured form of church organisation, maintained that civil magistrates should have no power at all in religious matters, that ministry should rely on freewill offerings, and that in each parish the pastor should be chosen by his own parishioners." The footnote to the Signet edition of the play talks of Browne as a "reformer who advocated the separation of church and state" and tells us that Sir Andrew's word "politician" means schemer.

Maria tends to be a good judge of character. She expands Olivia's accusation of "self-love".

> The devil, a puritan that he is, or anything, con-
> stantly, but a time-pleaser, an affectioned ass that cons
> state without book and utters it by great swathes; the
> best persuaded of himself, so crammed, as he thinks,

with excellencies, that it is his grounds of faith that all
that look on him love him

> (Act II, scene 3, 140-5)

In other words, he's sycophantic, affected, aping his betters by stuffing himself full of punctiliously memorised courtly gestures and phrases and with such a high estimation of his own worth that he believes everyone must automatically concur. These are hardly the qualities of a Puritan. It is Pride of the Seven Deadly Sins that dominates his character. Shakespeare is deliberately endowing a 'Puritan' with traits that are uncharacteristic, in order to show up hypocrisy. He is setting him up for a fall.

And when it comes it is extremely comic, both verbally and visually. What Malvolio is guilty of, as Maria rightly claimed, is daring to expect to move up the social ladder, to become at one with his betters. He already thinks he's top dog, claiming Olivia "uses me with a more exalted respect than anyone else that follows her". In his own words, he aspires "To be Count Malvolio." Greenblatt makes the point, "what is ridiculed in Malvolio ... is not simply ill-nature or puritanical severity but rather the dream of acting the part of a gentleman." It has nothing to do with love – love of Olivia for her beauty or the qualities of her mind: what he is after is raised status and the power it gives to treat 'inferiors' with contempt and disdain. His hubris reminds one of those men with aspirations who were on the move in Elizabethan times, threatening the social order. "Some are born great, some achieve greatness, and some have greatness thrust upon them." Though presented as preposterous in the play, and thought dangerous by most at the time, moving up the ladder was possible.

The action of the play relies much upon the relationship between servants and their employers. Viola, of gentle parentage, perforce comes down the ladder some rungs to become a servant to Orsino alongside Curio and Valentine, whom she/he seemingly outshines. Olivia relies on Maria and Fabian to keep her house in some semblance of order, and Feste to entertain her. One can well say that servants in this play make it possible for their betters to luxuriate in their particular kinds of self-indulgence. That said, they are also seen to be active in subverting them – even if, ironically, they do end up reaffirming the status quo.

Malvolio falls into a trap which not only humiliates him into overstepping "the modest limits of order" (as well as causing him to behave bizarrely and juggle with words and phrases he barely understands, forcing them to mean what he desires them to mean, but in the process betraying him into unwitting obscenities) but ends up imprisoning him as a madman. It is notable that Olivia feels pity for him in his humiliation. This is reinforced by Maria's statement that "My lady would not lose him for more than I'll say". Do we get the same impression of charity from Toby's remark "we must deal gently with him"? How do we square "special care" and "deal gently" with the treatment Malvolio is subjected to, and during which he is further baited by Feste as Sir Topas. Confinement in a dark room, we may recall, was thought suitable treatment for madness. If this is the case then we need to broaden our definition of madness and perhaps realistically accept the Elizabethan terror of being possessed by the devil. Are Olivia, Maria, Toby and Feste perhaps seriously trying to save his soul? Are they fearful of contagion? Or does Shakespeare simply overdo the joke? And if so, why does he, after Fabian's ameliorative lines encouraging us to "pluck on laughter than revenge", have Malvolio declare "I'll be revenged on the whole pack of you!" and Olivia say "He hath been most notoriously abused"? Why does he give him verse for the first time in the play? Are we to put any faith in the Duke's "entreat him to a peace"? Perhaps. But modern playgoers at least inevitably feel that the "joy and benevolence" of the ending has been clouded. In Middleton Murry's words, "Malvolio should have been more malevolent to deserve all his punishment". It could be said in mitigation that Maria acts the devil's part in seducing him from his wits. Whether the devil in Malvolio has been exorcised remains an open question.

We talked earlier of justice-in-the-world and poetic justice. Poetic justice arranges comeuppances, the whirligig of time bringing in its revenges; it also acts aesthetically as a making of satisfying patterns, ties things up neatly. But Shakespeare doesn't seem to have quite done this. And he points to a future outside the play: we are left to imagine the possible results of Orsino's order to bring Malvolio back "He hath not told us of the captain yet". Is he likely to be pacified? Are the couples likely to make good marriages, given the sexual ambiguities that we've been witness to? Impossible of course to answer but it is not invalid to ask. Additionally, we may ask what is the purpose of Feste's song which also takes us outside the play.

Perhaps Lamb is right in saying we should not let his "infirmity" shade his virtues. How far can we go along with Lamb's feelings of a "tragic interest"?

> That Malvolio was meant to be represented as possessing estimable qualities, the expression of the Duke, in his anxiety to have him reconciled, almost infers (*sic*). 'Pursue him, and entreat him to a peace.' Even in his abused state of chains and darkness, a sort of greatness seems never to desert him. He argues highly and well with the supposed Sir Topas, and philosophises gallantly upon his straw. There must be some shadow of worth about the man.

It cannot be denied that Malvolio's suffering is real nor that it releases a dark spirit into the supposedly sunny ending of the play, a spirit that Feste's final song seems to confirm.

13

All is Semblative a Woman's Part

The boys in Shakespeare's company must have been extremely talented. Most of the women's parts written for them are extensive and taxing. No one provides such full and exacting parts for female characters again until we get to Ibsen.

In a sense this is Viola's play. As Hazlitt says, "The great and secret charm of *Twelfth Night* is the character of Viola". In boy-actor terms, she is a walking parody. As a young woman, she impresses us in the way she copes with being the victim of a shipwreck, the supposed loss of her brother, and by the way she tends to think of others before herself – her brother and the Captain, in whom she instantly recognises worth. As a woman disguised, she carries off the deception convincingly, right up to the last moment. The play continually tests her 'wit' and she generally comes through without compromise. She is by no means subservient in the presence of Olivia, giving as good as she gets, and is able to speak more or less on equal terms with Feste. Her soliloquies show her thoughtful and resourceful. In her we see the way reason might be used to govern a life. And she brings about changes in other people's lives – we don't need to restate how she so obviously affects Olivia but we should note that she brings about subtle changes in the Duke. Of her description of the old and antique song which "gives a very echo to the seat/Where love is thron'd" Muir goes as far as to suggest that

> Orsino recognises that Cesario must have been in love. And,
> for the first time in the play, he is roused to take an interest in
> something other than his own emotions.

And as the conversation in this scene develops he "recognises that men's fancies are 'more giddy' than women's are"; and with the story of Cesario's imaginary sister:

> Orsino is again taken out of himself sufficiently to ask if Cesario's sister had died of her love. When at the end of the play Cesario's sex is revealed, Orsino remembers this story and Cesario's confession that she would never love a woman as much as she loved him, and he proposes marriage.

Middleton Murry, declaring Viola "but a girl", makes the comment: "This girl is older, if not in years, then in experience, than Beatrice or Rosalind or Portia."

Olivia too is a strong character temporarily and absurdly infected with excessive grief. She has, until their deaths, been dependant on men – her father and, particularly it seems, her brother. Now an heiress and a Countess, she is left to cope with a large estate and an unruly uncle of no help to her at all, and his feeble-minded sidekick, Aguecheek. Ostensibly she has her handmaid Maria, her steward Malvolio and the servant Fabian to rely on. And there's Feste, whose job is to try and put his mistress psychologically back on an even keel. In the play's terms, she is to all intents and purposes the equal of the Duke. She is decisive and practical in arranging her betrothal to Sebastian:

> Blame not this haste of mine. If you mean well,
> Now go with me and with this holy man
> Into the chantry by; there before him
> And underneath that consecrated roof
> Plight me the full assurance of your faith,
> That my most jealous and too doubtful soul
> May live at peace.
>
> (Act IV, scene 3, 22-8)

She cannot believe her luck but she is shrewd enough to have lined up and primed ("He shall conceal it") the holy man and to get the Church's seal of approval to make things official and binding:

> Then lead the way, good father, and heavens so shine
> That they may fairly note this act of mine!
>
> (Act IV, scene 3, 34-5)

In terms of the divided self (remember Antonio's "How have you made division of yourself?") and the languages she uses, she shows that behind her vow and her coy withdrawal from life there is a feisty woman only too eager to get out. It is better, Muir remarks, for the actor playing her to be "unconscious, or only partly conscious, that she is putting on an act."

In fact you could cogently argue that Viola, Olivia and the pert, energetic Maria contradict the implied attitude to women the play evinces. Even Viola utters the conventional view ("Alas, our frailty is the cause, not we,/For such as we are made of, such we be.") But in being brought on stage as 'real' women coping with real problems, they subvert the idealised image of woman of the courtly love code that Orsino is addicted to; additionally, they have youth on their side; and they all get their man. On an aesthetic level at least, the play allows us to feel the hovering presence of the ideal of mutuality, the prospect of a "marriage of true minds". To go a stage further, we could even say the female characters in the play show the males up and that, having a more forceful presence, they end up in control.

As for the men: we have a madly doting Duke needing to wake up to his responsibilities and to discover what true love is; a pair of reprobate knights seemingly beyond learning anything (unless we believe that Toby's marriage redeems him); a pompous steward mocked out of countenance and court; the rather odd Fabian who is complicit in the tricking of Malvolio but who tries to smooth things at the end. They are not a sensible lot. On the other hand we have the good represented in the Captain and Antonio, men who may claim to have seen something of life, and Sebastian who, though still a youth, like his sister, marries (ironic if you think of Malvolio's aspirations to do the same) above him. And then there is Feste ...

14

Corrupter of Words

Part of Feste's skill resides in his mastery of ambiguity, of double meanings – in a word, in language. In interchanges of wit he has to win. It's part of the job description. Elizabethan language is extraordinarily flexible and rich in meanings. Indeed, as we said earlier, because of the hierarchically arranged correspondences their world-view was made up of, their way of thinking was more analogical than ours. This also helps to account for the fact that *Twelfth Night* constantly draws on meanings that derive from parallels, contrasts, as well as the ripple-outward effect of words. The Elizabethans were committed punsters, capable of using puns, not only frivolously or bawdily, but sometimes with intense seriousness, as we saw earlier when we noted Viola's Illyria/Elysium wordplay.

We have also noted that most of the characters speak with at least two voices – the voice of pretence and the voice of their 'true' selves. It is this ambivalence and the tension between 'pretend' and 'real' selves that allow us to make judgements about them. It is what activates the play and is further exploited in confusions arising from cross-dressing and various other forms of disguise. What *seems* as opposed to what *is*. "How have you made division of yourself?"

The play then may be said to belong to those who are in control of language and consequently in control of their own realities.

Toby tends to use puns as evasion. He picks up words and twists them to mean something quite different from their intended meaning, something that suits his self-seeking or that pushes meaning aside altogether. For example, Maria's "exception" in Act I, scene 3, turns into the legal jargon of "let her except before excepted". Then to her word "confine" he replies "I'll confine myself no finer than I am". It is a typical refusal to take anything seriously. Maria too can pick up on a word and turn it to something else – for example Toby's estimation of Aguecheek as having "all the good gifts of nature" sparks her into "He hath indeed all, most natural" meaning like a natural fool, an idiot. But her 'wit' here is nearer to that of Feste – i.e. a way of declaring a truth. With Aguecheek when he enters, we find a different response to words – the dull-witted misconstruing or ignorance of meanings. Sir Andrew has no comprehension whatsoever of the word "accost", which Toby explains by means of synonyms: "front her, board her, woo her, assail her", indicating that to him "accost" has a deliberate sexual undercurrent. This titillates Maria if it doesn't Aguecheek, since we quickly find her pursuing it with her invitation for him to bring his "hand to the buttery bar", meaning her breasts. And he has no idea what is being implied in her word "dry". "What's your jest?" he ingenuously asks, unaware that she is implying he is impotent. The sexual pulse of this scene continues in Toby's comments on Sir Andrew's straight yellow hair:

> … it hangs like flax on a distaff; and
> I hope to see a huswife take thee between her legs and
> spin it off.
>
> (Act I, scene 3, 97-9)

Also in this scene we find Toby typically flippant with Andrew's assertion he "can cut a caper". In Toby's mind "caper" becomes capon and leads him to say "And I can cut the mutton to it". As caper suggests a spice as well having to do with dancing, it is also possible that the word "mustard" lies behind "mutton". Two scenes later we hear Toby turn "lethargy" into "lechery". It is useful to note that conversations between Toby and Aguecheek tend to be rooted in physicalities, in the sensual, the appetites – which is the quality Elizabethans considered animals excelled in. What we hear is language distorted by drunkenness. "'Tis a gentleman here – a plague o' these pickle-herring! How now, sot!" … "Let him be the devil and he will, I care not. Give me faith, say I. Well, it's all one." Drink = madness = possession = drowning. Feste immediately establishes this equation for us in his conversation with Olivia. The point is that we recognise the truth of it from the way it causes language to unhinge.

Malvolio too attempts to speak with something of Feste's manner:

OLIVIA What kind o' man is he?
MALVOLIO Why, of mankind.
OLIVIA What manner of man?
MALVOLIO Of very ill manner;

(Act I, scene 5, 145-8)

The effect is negative, denigratory, the imposition of his will on the situation. Ironically, as we have noted, this only makes the Countess more eager to see Orsino's messenger for herself.

As for Malvolio – he too lets his language (the dignity it allows him to profess) become infected. His responses to the forged letter turn him into one of fancy's shapes and make him "high fantastical". He takes a flight of fancy and puts on show what Maria had said of him, that he "cons state without book and utters it by great swarths". Not only that, he is made to sound oddly similar to Aguecheek in coming out with things the full meaning of which he is blithely unaware. In other words, to play the fool. There is a kind of onomatopoeic punning in Malvolio's describing what he supposes to be Olivia's handwriting, he declares:

… These be
her very C's, her U's and her T's; and thus makes she
her great P's. It is, in contempt of question, her hand.

(Act II, scene 5, 86-8)

He is blithely unconscious of the sexual and scatological meanings of this (he has already called himself Count). Not so the audience. It is a nice touch on the part of Shakespeare to have Aguecheek at this point naively ask "Her C's, her U's, and her T's? Why that?" Thus he is able to double the joke. It also recalls Toby's earlier "If thou hast not her i' th' end, call me Cut" – one meaning of which is gelding or horse whose tail has been docked, but it is not the one the audience immediately hears. Malvolio gets carried deeper into the linguistic trap in his attempt to solve the "fustian riddle" of:

I may command where I adore;
But silence, like a Lucrece' knife,

66

With bloodless stroke my heart doth gore;
M.O.A.I. doth sway my life.

(Act II, scene 5, 103-6)

We cannot believe Olivia, even speaking "in starts distractedly", could be capable of such banality. And yet Malvolio pursues it with fine pedantry:

'I may command where I adore.' Why, she
may command me. I serve her; she is my lady. Why,
this is evident to any formal capacity. There is no ob-
struction in this. And the end: what should that alpha-
betical position portend? If I could make that resemble
something in me ...'

(Act II, scene 5, 113-18)

In the event he is as gulled as Aguecheek. In Act III, scene 2, Maria is to say of him "Yond gull Malvolio is turned heathen.") In this scene 5 we are again aware of different kinds of language at work: Malvolio is given licence to think better of himself than he is and this is highlighted by the comments of the onlookers: Toby's abusive oubursts ("Fire and brimstone" ... "Bolts and shackles"), the bafflements of Andrew ("I knew 'twas I, for many do call me fool"), and Fabian's sideline cheering ("This wins him, liver and all"). The same may be said of them in the scenes involving the duel where a Quixotic chivalry and empty bravado are on exhibition – further illustration of the disparity between reality and pretence. In other words the characters become walking parodies, affecting attitudes to the processes of combat not dissimilar to the postures towards courtly love adopted by Orsino.

15

Nay, I Am for All Waters

the most difficult character in comedy is the fool,
and he who plays the part must be no simpleton.
(Cervantes, *Don Quixote*)

Allowed Fools are neither literary invention nor a piece of circus. Until well after Shakespeare's death Fools were still attached to noble houses. They were a social phenomenon – men who made their precarious living through the dextrous employment of their wits. They needed intelligence and skill and could, if thought to be up not to standard, be subjected to rebuke and harsh punishment. Feste enters the play on a threat of hanging for being absent without leave or – something equally bad – as Maria suggests "to be turned away – is not that as good as a hanging to you?"

Behind Allowed Fools stretches a long history of regarding deformed people, halfwits, dwarves as pets and/or objects of fun, though sometimes also with awe. What we called a 'natural' earlier (when talking about Aguecheek) was often in early times regarded with awe, since from their mouths – as from the mouths of babes and sucklings – might come inspired utterance. Hence a connection between Fools and wisdom and truth-telling – seen so potently at work in *Twelfth Night* and *Lear*.

It was up until 1599, the same year it is thought he wrote both *As You Like It* and *Twelfth Night*, that Shakespeare's comic roles had been played first by Dick Tarlton and then Will Kemp. In 1599 Kemp, who played the knockabout parts of Dogberry and Bottom, was replaced by Robert Armin. With Armin, as we said earlier, a subtler kind of comic writing was possible. In addition, Armin could sing. It was Armin who acted Touchstone, Feste and the Fool in *Lear*.

Armin was a conscientious comic actor; in writing for him

Shakespeare obviously felt comfortable. The fact that Armin published three books on his art testifies to his professional commitment and integrity.

Our first meeting with Feste finds him in the company of Olivia's lady-in-waiting, Maria, and it is quickly obvious that they are companions in wit. She can readily answer him back in kind. To his saying he is "resolved on two points" she gives the witty response "That if one break, the other will hold; or if both break, your gaskins fall", which Feste acknowledges with:

> Apt, in good faith, very apt. Well, go thy way, if
> Sir Toby would leave drinking, thou wert as witty
> a piece of Eve's flesh as any in Illyria.
>
> (Act I, scene 5, 24-6)

As Viola is to realise, Feste has learnt to adjust the quality of his wit to the company he is in. As Olivia's professional Fool, his job is to entertain her. He has to rely on a degree of sufferance; she is nowhere as censorious as her steward. Feste hopes for her respect. She tells Malvolio, with Feste present, that "There is no slander in an allowed fool, though he do nothing but rail" and, turning a stern eye on Malvolio, says "nor no railing in a known discreet man, though he do nothing but reprove". But this respect isn't necessarily guaranteed: he has to take risks to obtain it.

With Toby he simply joins in the fun, mostly speaking nonsense – for example:

> I did impetticoat thy gratillity; for Malvolio's nose
> is no whipstock, my lady has a white hand, and the
> Myrmidons are no bottle-ale houses.
>
> (Act II, scene 3, 25-7)

What he really adds to their company is song; they each pay him sixpence for his rendition of 'O mistress mine':

> FESTE Would you have a love song, or a song of good life?
> SIR TOBY A love song! A love song!
> SIR ANDREW Ay, ay, I care not for good life.
>
> (Act II, scene 3, 34-6)

What Aguecheek means here by "good life" is the Puritan idea of it – the suppression of the pleasure principle – at the same time it makes him sound as though he doesn't really like enjoying himself. In other words he makes a hypocrite of himself without knowing he's doing so. To him and Toby 'O mistress mine' is probably a bawdy song. Feste plays with Toby, Andrew and Maria as one might with children (though I have seen productions that try to show he's just as bad, as frivolous as they are). He indulges them:

> SIR TOBY My lady's a – Cataian; we are – politicians;
>   Malvolio's a – Peg-a-Ramsey, and (*he sings*)
>   Three merry men be we!
>   Am I not consanguineous? Am I not of her blood?
>   Tilly-vally! 'Lady'! (*he sings*)
>   There dwelt a man in Babylon, lady, lady –
> FESTE Beshrew me, the knight's in admirable fooling.
> SIR ANDREW Ay, he does well enough if he be disposed, and
>   so do I too. He does it with a better grace, but I do
>   it more natural.
>
> (Act II, scene 3, 73-82)

But his sympathies are with them when it comes to Malvolio.

He adjusts to the Duke's self-indulgent mood by singing him the deeply mournful "Come away, come away, death" and takes his money and bids the Duke adieu with the barbed words "Now the melancholy god protect thee."

He and Viola get on well together, at the beginning of Act III, in their discussion of language. Like Maria, Viola takes him seriously and is able to speak with him on equal terms. She remarks that "They that dally nicely with words may quickly make them wanton" – which we can use as a yardstick in assessing character. Words are the tools of his trade and he complains that words have become "very rascals since bonds disgraced them". The exact meaning of this is uncertain but it clearly carries the notion that Feste's occupation is becoming more difficult to perform. (Has this sentiment come out of discussions with the thoughtful Armin?) His view of his own profession is realistic and sceptical:

> VIOLA Art not thou the Lady Olivia's fool?
> FESTE No indeed, sir, the Lady Olivia has no folly. She will

keep no fool, sir, till she be married, and fools are as
like husbands as pilchers are to herrings; the husband's
the bigger. I am indeed not her fool, but her corrupter
of words.

(Act III, scene 1, 30-5)

The banter is still at work but with Viola it is on a more serious
level than with others. However, the last phrase is too difficult for
her to make a comeback. She changes the subject: "I saw thee late at
the Count Orsino's." Feste has raised the stakes and in doing so has
left us with the sort of questions about language Eliot raised in *Four
Quartets*:

> Words strain,
> Crack and sometimes break, under the burden,
> Under tension, slip, slide, perish,
> Decay with imprecision, will not stay in place,
> Will not stay still. Shrieking voices
> Scolding, mocking, or merely chattering,
> Always assail them.

Perhaps Feste loses some of our respect when he plays ("I will
dissemble") the part of Sir Topas – though he does admit to being
uncomfortable in the role) but remember it is he who is persuaded of
Malvolio's sanity, bringing him the pen and paper that finally secures
release. In doing so he uses two voices – Topas' and his own:

MALVOLIO Sir Topas!
FESTE Maintain no words with him, good fellow. (*In own
voice*) Who, I, sir? Not I, sir! God buy you, good Sir
Topas! (*In priest's voice*) Marry, amen! (*In own voice*)
I will, sir, I will.
MALVOLIO Fool! Fool! Fool, I say!
FESTE Alas, sir, be patient. What say you sir? I am shent
for speaking to you.

(Act IV, scene 2, 98-105)

I am tempted to say this constitutes a parody of all the other two-
voice circumstances of the play. Talking of which, we should also
mention the obvious fact that the play uses both poetry and prose –
indeed mostly prose – and it is not simply as a matter of distinguishing

noble characters from the less-noble: all of the characters, with the exception of the holy man, at some stage are involved in speaking prose.

John Wain remarks that Feste's "cold eye sees through all pretence, and the play turns on pretences, conscious and unconscious". He is instrumental in affirming Malvolio's sanity and in awakening the principal characters to love – in which, as he perfectly understands, there "lies no plenty". As Wain says, "Nothing is hidden from him, the onlooker who sees more of the game than the players". It sometimes feels as though he has walked up out of the audience to mingle with the characters. Because "Foolery, sir, does walk about the orb like the sun; it shines everywhere" he is of everywhere and nowhere. In the words of Middleton Murry:

> There is a strange aloofness in Feste: he is attached … to nobody. He is woven in and out of the play like a careless wraith. Nothing matters to him. If he is turned away, 'let summer bear it out'. His fooling has a different flavour from the fooling of any other fool. It is almost metaphysical in its aloofness. And … it seems natural that he should be, as he is, more unblushing in his demands for money than any other of Shakespeare's fools. He has no illusion about his own precariousness. It sorts with this that at one moment he appears to be abrupt and careless of his reward – after singing 'Come away, death'. 'There's for thy pains', says the Duke. 'No pains, sir, I take pleasure in singing', says Feste. At all events, it is clear that he does take pleasure In singing – more truly than any other character in a play which begins and ends in music, and is saturated with it.

At the end of it is he who is left onstage – as if, like Prospero, the play has been all his after all, as in a sense it has. Our revels now are ended. Well, not quite. It's a nice conceit, for as we know it was customary for the cast to reappear at the end of a play and perform a vigorous dance.

16

The Whirligig of Time

It is one of the play's ironies that, belonging to a woman intent on abjuring the sight and company of men, Olivia's house attracts them in the final scene like flies. As well as those already there (Toby, Andrew, Fabian, Malvolio and Feste), others come bundling in (the Duke, Curio, attendant lords, Sebastian, Antonio, the arresting officers, a priest – not forgetting Cesario and Feste's doubling up as Sir Topas). Poor Granville-Barker considered it so much of a chaos that he could only imagine in it "scraps of the play (Shakespeare) first mean to write".

Meanwhile Olivia, thinking she has finally conquered Viola/ Cesario, has wasted no time in securing a betrothal to her presumably look-alike brother. Whether this peremptorily-made arrangement denotes the achieving of true love is an open question. Sebastian is equally peremptory: whether his assertion of constancy ("having sworn truth, ever will be true.") is to be trusted is again open. But let's not forget that we are in the tradition of romantic comedy going back to the Roman Terence and Plautus where such things happen. With this betrothal the tangled knot has become even more tangled.

The final scene is a fast-moving concatenation of entrances and exits, skilfully arranged for maximum comic-drama effect. It opens inconsequentially enough with Feste's refusal of Fabian's request to read Malvolio's letter. They are interrupted by the surprise invasion of Olivia's garden by Orsino and his retinue. So the letter is held in abeyance. Orsino's entrance surprises because we have grown accustomed to the idea of the Duke languishing at home and listening to mournful music. Now suddenly he has actively entered the real world. First there is a bit of banter with Feste, during which the jester utters the telling line "I profit in the knowledge of myself". It is something other characters are now heading for: the awakening out of self-love into the fresh air of self-knowledge, which makes them open to real love. The good side of Orsino is revealed in his generosity; but he is also shown as someone who cannot be pushed too far ("You can fool no more money out of me at this throw.") In this interchange with Feste we do not hear him, even gently, mocked.

The real world imposes itself further with the arrival of the arrested Antonio, instantly recognised by Viola ("Here comes the man, sir, that did rescue me.") He is also recognised by the Duke, who clearly has respect for him, even as an enemy ("very envy and the tongue of loss/Cried fame and honour on him"). Orsino is now being called upon to act with the responsibility incumbent upon him as ruler. Honour and its preservation are of paramount importance and what is being asserted here is the idea of true manliness – the contrast with which is to be found in the farrago of the duel. Viola also emphasises Antonio's kindness. He himself in his long speech confirms what is said of him, clueing Viola into thinking her brother is still alive. Into the middle of all this stride Olivia and her retinue; and immediately Orsino reverts to courtly hyperbole. But, face-to-face with the real-life subject of his adorations, he is required to take her real-life rejection of him on board. Her position is strengthened by the knowledge that she is already betrothed – or so she thinks – to one of the people standing there. Orsino is furious. He is experiencing real emotions at last, even if they drive him to murderous and vengeful thoughts. In his anger, he makes to go, taking Viola/Cesario with him. He/she is delighted (Muir says that for a moment she loses her common sense) that Orsino now seems to be free.

Mistaken for Sebastian, Cesario is flummoxed by Olivia's "Cesario, husband, stay!" The Countess, with a whole batch of ironies, given the themes of the play as we have tried to outline them, says:

> Alas, it is the baseness of thy fear
> That makes thee strangle thy propriety.
> Fear not, Cesario, take thy fortunes up.
> Be that thou know'st thou art, and then thou art
> As great as that thou fear'st.
>
> (Act V, scene 1, (144-8)

As Feste says, "Some are born great, some achieve greatness, and some have greatness thrown upon them."

The priest enters to confirm the betrothal and Orsino's fury is compounded:

> O thou dissembling cub! What wilt thou be
> When time hath sowed a grizzle on thy case?
> Or will not else thy craft so quickly grow
> That thine own trip shall be thine overthrow?
> Farewell, and take her; but direct thy feet
> Where thou and I henceforth may never meet.
>
> (Act V, scene 1, 162-7)

Now enter Sir Andrew Aguecheek with the results of the duel: "He's broke my head across, and he's given Sir Toby a bloody coxcomb too" – pointing to Cesario. No wonder Granville-Barker uses the word "chaos". But it is an artfully engineered chaos and made worse by the arrival of Toby. Now it is Olivia who has to face realities and deal with them. She too is on a learning curve. Toby is sent off to be attended to but not before he exclaims "I hate a drunken rogue", referring to the surgeon who Feste says, with some poetic irony, is drunk. Is Toby's exclamation simply anger or is it a sign of reformation? And can the same questions be asked of his rejection of Aguecheek: "Will you help? An asshead, and a coxcomb, and a knave – a thin-faced knave, a gull!"

Now Sebastian enters the mayhem and with him comes our first glimpse of a resolution. It is an intensely visual theatrical moment, that is if Viola and he can be made to look like identical twins. The Duke expresses his amazement by thinking he's seeing an optical illusion:

> One face, one voice, one habit, and two persons!
> A natural perspective, that is and is not.
>
> (Act V, scene 1, 213-4)

The audience rejoices in this on-stage bafflement, largely because it is in possession of knowledge the characters are innocent of. It is not outcome we are uncertain of but the ins and outs by which it is eventually arrived at. Malvolio is not the only one to whom the words "Alas, poor fool, how they have baffled thee!" are applicable.

Sebastian apologises to Olivia for wounding Toby, claiming self-defence: "had it been the brother of my blood/I must have done no less, with wit and safety." Then he greets his bosom friend, Antonio, who exclaims "How have you made division of yourself?", which in seven words crystallises so much of what the play is about. The knot begins to untangle.

The twins are reunited but not before Viola, nervously thinking of the devil, says:

> If spirits can assume both form and suit
> You come to fright us.
>
> (Act V, scene 1, 232-3)

The Duke now remembers Cesario's "Thou shouldst never love woman like to me" and offers his hand. It is a strange moment and its ambivalences shouldn't be lost on us. Sebastian tells Olivia "You are betrothed both to a maid and man." It is the same with Orsino but stranger: he has yet to see Viola in all her feminine glory. There are some people who find this disturbing: Orsino professing love for someone who to all intents and purposes has the appearance of a boy, his "let me see thee in thy woman's weeds" and "when in other habits you are seen" sounding decidedly awkward. But then again we are within the world of romantic comedy where such things are allowed. Like licence to misrule.

There only remains the problem of Malvolio.

We expect romantic comedy to conclude with marriage or multiple marriages, solemn and at the same time joyful comings-together of couples when "each circumstance/Of place, time, fortune do cohere and jump" and with the acquiring of a degree of self-knowledge. Given the tradition in which we are operating we don't allow ourselves to fret too much over the questions we posited earlier. Does it matter that Sebastian is whirlwinded into marriage or that Orsino is offering his hand to a boy playing the part of a young woman playing the part of a young man, with her double standing there too? The couples have arrived where we want them and they want to be – where we knew they were heading all along. The rest we take on trust. Or we keep reservations to ourselves – even if we find ourselves encouraged into a more sceptical frame of mind by Feste's final song. Who wants to spoil a happy ending? Well, maybe Shakespeare did – or at least temper it. There still remains the problem of Malvolio and how to get him out of the prison he is in. It is done by letter – but this time a letter that isn't feigned or forged; but genuine and sane. Through it he, in a sense, releases himself from imprisonment, aided and abetted by Feste.

This letter is read out – not without further attempts at wringing more amusement out of his plight. It is Olivia, whose regard for him, doesn't seem to falter, who insists on a fair hearing, telling Feste, who had tried to satirise Malvolio in his loud reading out of it. The Duke is impressed: "this," he says, "savours not much of distraction." The letter, though a complaining one, is rational and not without dignity. He has every right to be angry and to demand explanations. Olivia responds fairly, saying:

> ... when we know the grounds and authors of it,
> Thou shalt be both the plaintiff and the judge
> Of thine own cause.
>
> (Act V, scene 1, 351-3)

It – and Fabian's confession which includes a plea for the adopting of an attitude of leniency and humour, and Feste's confession ("I was one, sir, in this interlude") plus an assertion of poetic justice ("the whirligig of time brings in his revenges") – fail to satisfy Malvolio, who exits famously with the words "I'll be revenged on the whole pack of you!" How much faith can we put in the Duke's "Pursue him and entreat him to a peace", to have him come back and tie up a loose end : "He hath not told us of the Captain yet" – meaning Viola's friend last met in Act I, scene 2?

For most people the righteous anger of Malvolio clouds the happy ending, the prospect offered in Olivia's "One day shall crown th'alliance on't." Well, we will never know about Malvolio nor the Captain nor the fate of Sir Andrew (except to suppose he goes home worse off than when he came). As for Toby, he's ahead of them all, already married.

Epilogue – Hey, Ho

They all leave the stage heading into circumstances outside the play which we can have no knowledge of, leaving Feste on the bare, un-peopled stage to occupy that moment between action and applause and bring the performance to an end,. And he does so in a way that's unexpected, with a song of bitter experience, the result of taking an unblinkered look at life. It starts with the innocent vision of the tiny child, where nothing seems upsetting. Growing up changes this: life gets cruel, you have to learn to defend yourself in a world of fools and robbers; then marriage comes and, too proud, too boastful ('swaggering'), you make a mess of it; finally you end up in old age, drunk with the rest of the tosspots. The final verse offers a cosmic perspective, suggesting this is the way things have been before and will be again. Then comes the signal for applause 'But that's all one, our play is done' and we realise we have been eased out of the comic enchantment the play has engaged us in for however long it has taken. 'That's all one' is a sentiment we have heard several times in the play. Maybe what it asks of us is a stoical acceptance – a way of saying never mind, it doesn't really matter all that much, it's only been a play, you can go home now … hang on though, we've got a dance for you.

Bibliography

Maurice Ashley, *England in the Seventeenth Century* (Penguin, 1952)

Harley Granville-Barker, *Prefaces to Shakespeare* (Batsford, 1963)

Jonathan Bate, *The Genius of Shakespeare* (Picador, 1997)

William Blake, *Complete Poems* (Penguin, 1977)

Eric Blom, *Music in England* (Penguin, 1947)

Robert Burton, *The Anatomy of Melancholy* (Kessinger, 1998)

A J. Denomy, *The Heresy of Courtly Love* (D.X. McMullen, New York, 1947)

Waverly Fitzgerald, *School of Seasons*
http://www.schooloftheseasons.com/twelfthnight.html

T.S. Eliot, *The Complete Poems and Plays of T.S. Eliot* (Faber & Faber, 1969)

Stephen Greenblatt, *Will in the World* (Jonathan Cape, 2004)

John Hale, *The Civilisation of Europe in the Renaissance* (Harper Collins, 1993)

William Hazlitt, *Characters of Shakespeare's Plays* (Taylor & Hessey, 1818)

Anthony Holden, *William Shakespeare – His Life and His Work* (Abacus, 1999)

Ben Jonson, *Three Comedies* (Penguin, 1977)

Charles Lamb, *Elia, Essays which have appeared under his signature in The London Magazine*, (Taylor & Hessey, 1823)

Christopher Marlowe, *The Complete Plays* (Penguin, 1969)

Andrew Marvell, *Complete Poems* (Dent, 1984)

Kenneth Muir, *Shakespeare's Comic Sequence* (Liverpool University Press, 1979)

John Middleton Murry, *Shakespeare* (Jonathan Cape, 1935)

ed. Alex Preminger, *Princeton Encyclopedia of Poetry and Poetics* (Macmillan, 1975)

George Puttenham, *Arte of English Poesie* (Scolar P, 1968)

Roman Selden, *Practising Theory and Reading Literature* (Harvester Wheatsheaf, 1989)

Philip Sidney, *A Defence of Poetry* (OUP, 1971)

Martin Seymour-Smith, ed. *Shakespeare's Sonnets* (Greenwich Exchange, 2001)

T.J.B. Spencer, ed. *Elizabethan Love Stories* (Penguin Shakespeare Library, 1968)

E.M.W. Tillyard, *The Elizabethan World Picture* (Cambridge, 1943)

John Wain, *The Living World of Shakespeare* (Penguin, 1964)

John Dover Wilson, *Shakespeare's Happy Comedies* (Faber & Faber, 1962)

My source for Hazlitt, Lamb, Granville-Barker and Dover Wilson is The Signet edition of the play.

All other quotations are from the New Penguin Shakespeare edition of the play (ISBN: 0-141-01470-9).

GREENWICH EXCHANGE BOOKS

STUDENT GUIDE LITERARY SERIES

The Greenwich Exchange Student Guide Literary Series is a collection of critical essays of major or contemporary serious writers in English and selected European languages. The series is for the student, the teacher and 'common readers' and is an ideal resource for libraries. The *Times Educational Supplement* praised these books, saying, "The style of [this series] has a pressure of meaning behind it. Readers should learn from that … If art is about selection, perception and taste, then this is it."

(ISBN prefix 1-871551- applies)
All books are paperbacks unless otherwise stated

The series includes:
W.H. Auden by Stephen Wade (36-6)
Honoré de Balzac by Wendy Mercer (48-X)
William Blake by Peter Davies (27-7)
The Brontës by Peter Davies (24-2)
Robert Browning by John Lucas (59-5)
Lord Byron by Andrew Keanie (83-9)
Samuel Taylor Coleridge by Andrew Keanie (64-1)
Joseph Conrad by Martin Seymour-Smith (18-8)
William Cowper by Michael Thorn (25-0)
Charles Dickens by Robert Giddings (26-9)
Emily Dickinson by Marnie Pomeroy (68-4)
John Donne by Sean Haldane (23-4)
Ford Madox Ford by Anthony Fowles (63-3)
The Stagecraft of Brian Friel by David Grant (74-9)
Robert Frost by Warren Hope (70-6)
Thomas Hardy by Sean Haldane (33-1)
Seamus Heaney by Warren Hope (37-4)
Joseph Heller by Anthony Fowles (84-6)
Gerard Manley Hopkins by Sean Sheehan (77-3)
James Joyce by Michael Murphy (73-0)
Philip Larkin by Warren Hope (35-8)
Laughter in the Dark – The Plays of Joe Orton by Arthur Burke (56-0)
Poets of the First World War by John Greening (79-X)
Philip Roth by Paul McDonald (72-2)
Shakespeare's *A Midsummer Night's Dream* by Matt Simpson (86-2)
Shakespeare's *Macbeth* by Matt Simpson (69-2)

Shakespeare's *Othello* by Matt Simpson (71-4)
Shakespeare's *The Tempest* by Matt Simpson (75-7)
Shakespeare's *Twelfth Night* by Matt Simpson (86-2)
Shakespeare's *The Winter's Tale* by John Lucas (80-3)
Shakespeare's **Non-Dramatic Poetry** by Martin Seymour-Smith (22-6)
Shakespeare's **Sonnets** by Martin Seymour-Smith (38-2)
Tobias Smollett by Robert Giddings (21-8)
Dylan Thomas by Peter Davies (78-1)
Alfred, Lord Tennyson by Michael Thorn (20-X)
William Wordsworth by Andrew Keanie (57-9)
W.B. Yeats by John Greening (34-X)

LITERATURE & BIOGRAPHY

Matthew Arnold and 'Thyrsis' *by Patrick Carill Connolly*
Matthew Arnold (1822-1888) was a leading poet, intellect and aesthete of
the Victorian epoch. He is now best known for his strictures as a literary
and cultural critic, and educationist. After a long period of neglect, his
views have come in for a re-evaluation. Arnold's poetry remains less well
known, yet his poems and his understanding of poetry, which defied the
conventions of his time, were central to his achievement.
The author traces Arnold's intellectual and poetic development, showing
how his poetry gathers its meanings from a lifetime's study of European
literature and philosophy. Connolly's unique exegesis of 'Thyrsis' draws
upon a wide-ranging analysis of the pastoral and its associated myths in
both classical and native cultures. This study shows lucidly and in detail
how Arnold encouraged the intense reflection of the mind on the subject
placed before it, believing in " … the all importance of the choice of the
subject, the necessity of accurate observation; and subordinate character
of expression."
Patrick Carill Connolly gained his English degree at Reading University
and taught English literature abroad for a number of years before returning
to Britain. He is now a civil servant living in London.
2004 • 180 pages • ISBN 1-871551-61-7

The Author, the Book and the Reader *by Robert Giddings*
This collection of essays analyses the effects of changing technology and
the attendant commercial pressures on literary styles and subject matter.
Authors covered include Charles Dickens, Tobias Smollett, Mark Twain,
Dr Johnson and John le Carré.
1991 • 220 pages • illustrated • ISBN 1-871551-01-3

Norman Cameron *by Warren Hope*

Cameron's poetry was admired by Auden; celebrated by Dylan Thomas; valued by Robert Graves. He was described by Martin Seymour-Smith as "one of ... the most rewarding and pure poets of his generation ..." and is at last given a full-length biography. This eminently sociable man, who had periods of darkness and despair, wrote little poetry by comparison with others of his time, but always of a consistently high quality – imaginative and profound.

Warren Hope is a poet, a critic and university lecturer. He lives and works in Philadelphia, where he raised his family.

2000 • 226 pages • ISBN 1-871551-05-6

Aleister Crowley and the Cult of Pan *by Paul Newman*

Few more nightmarish figures stalk English literature than Aleister Crowley (1875-1947), poet, magician, mountaineer and agent provocateur. In this groundbreaking study, Paul Newman dives into the occult mire of Crowley's works and fishes out gems and grotesqueries that are by turns ethereal, sublime, pornographic and horrifying. Like Oscar Wilde before him, Crowley stood in "symbolic relationship to his age" and to contemporaries like Rupert Brooke, G.K. Chesterton and the Portuguese modernist, Fernando Pessoa. An influential exponent of the cult of the Great God Pan, his essentially 'pagan' outlook was shared by major European writers as well as English novelists like E.M. Forster, D.H. Lawrence and Arthur Machen.

Paul Newman lives in Cornwall. Editor of the literary magazine *Abraxas*, he has written over ten books.

2004 • 222 pages • ISBN 1-871551-66-8

John Dryden *by Anthony Fowles*

Of all the poets of the Augustan age, John Dryden was the most worldly. Anthony Fowles traces Dryden's evolution from 'wordsmith' to major poet. This critical study shows a poet of vigour and technical panache whose art was forged in the heat and battle of a turbulent polemical and pamphleteering age. Although Dryden's status as a literary critic has long been established, Fowles draws attention to his neglected achievements as a translator of poetry. He deals also with the less well-known aspects of Dryden's work – his plays and occasional pieces.

Born in London and educated at the Universities of Oxford and Southern California, Anthony Fowles began his career in film-making before becoming an author of film and television scripts and more than twenty books. Readers will welcome the many contemporary references to novels and film with which Fowles illuminates the life and work of this decisively influential English poetic voice.

2003 • 292 pages • ISBN 1-871551-58-7

The Good That We Do *by John Lucas*
John Lucas' book blends fiction, biography and social history in order to tell the story of his grandfather, Horace Kelly. Headteacher of a succession of elementary schools in impoverished areas of London, 'Hod' Kelly was also a keen cricketer, a devotee of the music hall, and included among his friends the great trade union leader Ernest Bevin. In telling the story of his life, Lucas has provided a fascinating range of insights into the lives of ordinary Londoners from the First World War until the outbreak of the Second World War. Threaded throughout is an account of such people's hunger for education, and of the different ways government, church and educational officialdom ministered to that hunger. *The Good That We Do* is both a study of one man and of a period when England changed, drastically and forever.

John Lucas is Professor Emeritus of the Universities of Loughborough and Nottingham Trent. He is the author of numerous works of a critical and scholarly nature and has published seven collections of poetry.

2001 • 214 pages • ISBN 1-871551-54-4

D.H. Lawrence: The Nomadic Years, 1919-1930 *by Philip Callow*
This book provides a fresh insight into Lawrence's art as well as his life. Candid about the relationship between Lawrence and his wife, it shows nevertheless the strength of the bond between them. If no other book persuaded the reader of Lawrence's greatness, this does.

Philip Callow was born in Birmingham and studied engineering and teaching before he turned to writing. He has published 14 novels, several collections of short stories and poems, a volume of autobiography, and biographies on the lives of Chekhov, Cezanne, Robert Louis Stevenson, Walt Whitman and Van Gogh all of which have received critical acclaim. His biography of D.H. Lawrence's early years, *Son and Lover*, was widely praised.

2006 • 226 pages • ISBN 1-871551-82-X

Liar! Liar!: Jack Kerouac – Novelist *by R.J. Ellis*
The fullest study of Jack Kerouac's fiction to date. It is the first book to devote an individual chapter to every one of his novels. *On the Road*, *Visions of Cody* and *The Subterraneans* are reread in-depth, in a new and exciting way. *Visions of Gerard* and *Doctor Sax* are also strikingly reinterpreted, as are other daringly innovative writings, like 'The Railroad Earth' and his "try at a spontaneous *Finnegans Wake*" – *Old Angel Midnight*. Neglected

writings, such as *Tristessa* and *Big Sur*, are also analysed, alongside better-known novels such as *Dharma Bums* and *Desolation Angels.*
R.J. Ellis is Senior Lecturer in English at Nottingham Trent University.
1999 • 294 pages • ISBN 1-871551-53-6

Musical Offering *by Yolanthe Leigh*
In a series of vivid sketches, anecdotes and reflections, Yolanthe Leigh tells the story of her growing up in the Poland of the 1930s and the Second World War. These are poignant episodes of a child's first encounters with both the enchantments and the cruelties of the world; and from a later time, stark memories of the brutality of the Nazi invasion, and the hardships of student life in Warsaw under the Occupation. But most of all this is a record of inward development; passages of remarkable intensity and simplicity describe the girl's response to religion, to music, and to her discovery of philosophy.
Yolanthe Leigh was formerly a Lecturer in Philosophy at Reading University.
2000 • 56 pages • ISBN: 1-871551-46-3

In Pursuit of Lewis Carroll *by Raphael Shaberman*
Sherlock Holmes and the author uncover new evidence in their investigations into the mysterious life and writing of Lewis Carroll. They examine published works by Carroll that have been overlooked by previous commentators. A newly-discovered poem, almost certainly by Carroll, is published here.
Amongst many aspects of Carroll's highly complex personality, this book explores his relationship with his parents, numerous child friends, and the formidable Mrs Liddell, mother of the immortal Alice. Raphael Shaberman was a founder member of the Lewis Carroll Society and a teacher of autistic children.
1994 • 118 pages • illustrated • ISBN 1-871551-13-7

Poetry in Exile: A study of the poetry of W.H. Auden, Joseph Brodsky & George Szirtes *by Michael Murphy* (266pp)
"Michael Murphy discriminates the forms of exile and expatriation with the shrewdness of the cultural historian, the acuity of the literary critic, and the subtlety of a poet alert to the ways language and poetic form embody the precise contours of experience. His accounts of Auden, Brodsky and Szirtes not only cast much new light on the work of these complex and rewarding poets, but are themselves a pleasure to read." *Stan Smith, Research Professor in Literary Studies, Nottingham Trent University.*
Michael Murphy is a poet and critic. He teaches English literature at Liverpool Hope University College.
2004 • 266 pages • ISBN 1-871551-76-5

POETRY

Adam's Thoughts in Winter *by Warren Hope*
Warren Hope's poems have appeared from time to time in a number of literary periodicals, pamphlets and anthologies on both sides of the Atlantic. They appeal to lovers of poetry everywhere. His poems are brief, clear, frequently lyrical, characterised by wit, but often distinguished by tenderness. The poems gathered in this first book-length collection counter the brutalising ethos of contemporary life, speaking of, and for, the virtues of modesty, honesty and gentleness in an individual, memorable way.
2000 • 46 pages • ISBN 1-871551-40-4

Baudelaire: Les Fleurs du Mal *Translated by F.W. Leakey*
Selected poems from *Les Fleurs du Mal* are translated with parallel French texts and are designed to be read with pleasure by readers who have no French as well as those who are practised in the French language.
F.W. Leakey was Professor of French in the University of London. As a scholar, critic and teacher he specialised in the work of Baudelaire for 50 years and published a number of books on the poet.
2001 • 152 pages • ISBN 1-871551-10-2

'The Last Blackbird' and other poems by Ralph Hodgson *edited and introduced by John Harding*
Ralph Hodgson (1871-1962) was a poet and illustrator whose most influential and enduring work appeared to great acclaim just prior to, and during, the First World War. His work is imbued with a spiritual passion for the beauty of creation and the mystery of existence. This new selection brings together, for the first time in 40 years, some of the most beautiful and powerful 'hymns to life' in the English language.
John Harding lives in London. He is a freelance writer and teacher and is Ralph Hodgson's biographer.
2004 • 70 pages • ISBN 1-871551-81-1

Lines from the Stone Age *by Sean Haldane*
Reviewing Sean Haldane's 1992 volume *Desire in Belfast*, Robert Nye wrote in *The Times* that "Haldane can be sure of his place among the English poets." This place is not yet a conspicuous one, mainly because his early volumes appeared in Canada, and because he has earned his living by other means than literature. Despite this, his poems have always had their circle of readers. The 60 previously unpublished poems of *Lines from the Stone Age* – "lines of longing, terror, pride, lust and pain" – may widen this circle.
2000 • 52 pages • ISBN 1-871551-39-0

Martin Seymour-Smith – Collected Poems *edited by Peter Davies* (180pp)
To the general public Martin Seymour-Smith (1928-1998) is known as a distinguished literary biographer, notably of Robert Graves, Rudyard Kipling and Thomas Hardy. To such figures as John Dover Wilson, William Empson, Stephen Spender and Anthony Burgess, he was regarded as one of the most independently-minded scholars of his generation, through his pioneering critical edition of Shakespeare's *Sonnets*, and his magisterial *Guide to Modern World Literature*.
To his fellow poets, Graves, James Reeves, C.H. Sisson and Robert Nye – he was first and foremost a poet. As this collection demonstrates, at the centre of the poems is a passionate engagement with Man, his sexuality and his personal relationships.
2006 • 182 pages • ISBN 1-871551-47-1

Shakespeare's Sonnets *by Martin Seymour-Smith*
Martin Seymour-Smith's outstanding achievement lies in the field of literary biography and criticism. In 1963 he produced his comprehensive edition, in the old spelling, of *Shakespeare's Sonnets* (here revised and corrected by himself and Peter Davies in 1998). With its landmark introduction and its brilliant critical commentary on each sonnet, it was praised by William Empson and John Dover Wilson. Stephen Spender said of him "I greatly admire Martin Seymour-Smith for the independence of his views and the great interest of his mind"; and both Robert Graves and Anthony Burgess described him as the leading critic of his time. His exegesis of the *Sonnets* remains unsurpassed.
2001 • 194 pages • ISBN 1-871551-38-2

The Rain and the Glass *by Robert Nye*
When Robert Nye's first poems were published, G.S. Fraser declared in the *Times Literary Supplement*: "Here is a proper poet, though it is hard to see how the larger literary public (greedy for flattery of their own concerns) could be brought to recognize that. But other proper poets – how many of them are left? – will recognize one of themselves."
Since then Nye has become known to a large public for his novels, especially *Falstaff* (1976), winner of the Hawthornden Prize and The Guardian Fiction Prize, and *The Late Mr Shakespeare* (1998). But his true vocation has always been poetry, and it is as a poet that he is best known to his fellow poets. "Nye is the inheritor of a poetic tradition that runs from Donne and Ralegh to Edward Thomas and Robert Graves," wrote James Aitchison in 1990, while the critic Gabriel Josipovici has described him as "one of the most interesting poets writing today, with a voice unlike that of any of his contemporaries".

This book contains all the poems Nye has written since his *Collected Poems* of 1995, together with his own selection from that volume. An introduction, telling the story of his poetic beginnings, affirms Nye's unfashionable belief in inspiration, as well as defining that quality of unforced truth which distinguishes the best of his work: "I have spent my life trying to write poems, but the poems gathered here came mostly when I was not."
2005 • 132 pages • ISBN 1-871551-41-2

Wilderness *by Martin Seymour-Smith*
This is Martin Seymour-Smith's first publication of his poetry for more than twenty years. This collection of 36 poems is a fearless account of an inner life of love, frustration, guilt, laughter and the celebration of others. He is best known to the general public as the author of the controversial and bestselling *Hardy* (1994).
1994 • 52 pages • ISBN 1-871551-08-0

BUSINESS

English Language Skills *by Vera Hughes*
If you want to be sure, (as a student, or in your business or personal life), that your written English is correct, this book is for you. Vera Hughes' aim is to help you to remember the basic rules of spelling, grammar and punctuation. 'Noun', 'verb', 'subject', 'object' and 'adjective' are the only technical terms used. The book teaches the clear, accurate English required by the business and office world. It coaches acceptable current usage and makes the rules easier to remember.
Vera Hughes was a civil servant and is a trainer and author of training manuals.
2002 • 142 pages • ISBN 1-871551-60-9

The Essential Accounting Dictionary of Key Financial Terms
by Linda Hodgson
This is a key aide for students seeking examination success in Accounting A-Level and GNVQ Advanced Business. It results from work with teachers and students and addresses common difficulties. Straightforward, easy to read definitions of key financial terms – which form the basis of understanding and better performance at tests and examination. There is a multiple choice quiz to crosscheck how much the student knows.
Linda Jane Hodgson, graduate in History and Politics, is a former Tax Inspector and qualified teacher. Professionally, she also advised accounting firms on taxation. She now teaches business and finance at a London college.
1999 • 150 pages • ISBN 1-871551-50-1